Historians for the Future
A History of the Indiana Junior Historical Society
1938–1998

HISTORIANS FOR THE FUTURE

*A History of the Indiana Junior Historical Society
1938 - 1998*

Kendal H. Gladish and Hester Anne Hale

Indiana Historical Bureau and Indiana Historical Society
Indianapolis 1999

Printed in the United States of America

The paper in this publication meets the minimum requirements of American National Standard for Information Sciences—Permanence of Paper for Printed Library Materials, ANSI Z39.48-1984

Library of Congress Cataloging-in-Publication Data
Gladish, Kendal H.
     Historians for the future : a history of the Indiana Junior Historical Society,
  1938–1998 / Kendal H. Gladish and Hester Anne Hale.
       p.   cm.
    ISBN 0-87195-133-9 (alk. paper)
     1. Indiana Junior Historical Society—History.   I. Hale, Hester Anne.   II. Title.
F521.G57   1999
977.2'006—dc21   99-21541
                                                CIP

Contents

Foreword   vii

Preface   xi

1. Pioneers to the Past   1

2. Retreat and Revival: The War Years   19

3. Members and Activities Multiply   29

4. New Clubs and State Events Unfold   49

5. Sustaining IJHS Beyond the Seventies   63

6. Leadership and Management Change at Fifty-Year Mark   81

7. Sixty Years Strong   93

Notes   109

Appendix   119

Index   121

Foreword

As far back as the 1930s, when the Marion High School History Club became the pioneer unit of the Indiana Junior Historical Society, the overriding theme was: studying history is fun.

Falling before a variety of imaginative and interactive projects, the sometimes-held notion that history studies should consist of memorizing dry, uninteresting dates began to disappear. In its place came the thrill of participating in dramatic, on-site recitations and reenactments that created a lively "here-and-now" element, which helped determine the future by interpreting the past.

Since that time, junior historical chapters have demonstrated an interest in community service that goes beyond the walls of the school buildings.

Throughout the state, the juniors have conducted architectural surveys, restored neglected cemeteries, replaced weather-worn markers, written and published local histories, conducted historic home tours, and created exhibits illustrating, for example, Hoosier history through postage stamps.

But in the beginning progress did not come easily. The Marion chapter attempted to organize, but its approach was new and untried. School closed for the summer with only nine members. But in its brief springtime existence, the chapter members began to learn history by listening to fascinating on-site recitals at the Mississinewa Battleground and the nearby Indian cemetery and church. Dr. Otho Winger, president of Manchester College and a former teacher at the Indian village school, and Ross Franklin Lockridge, Sr., of Bloomington, both powerful and dramatic speakers, were the magnets that inspired the students and set the stage for the ensuing successful year.

As the fall semester opened, students rushed to join. The new and dramatic "fun" approach was so appealing that more than seventy signed up for membership, and the officers, fearing the organization was getting out of hand, closed the rolls.

But the enthusiasm could not be contained. Before long the organization established an annual "Local History Week," which spotlighted the colorful history of Marion and Grant County. Local merchants enthusiastically donated display window space, and junior society members worked tirelessly to collect artifacts and photos of early Marion and display them attractively in the donated space. Other members wrote articles on selected historical subjects that the *Marion Chronicle* and *Marion Leader-Tribune* published, while still others sharpened their speaking skills and presented programs at weekly service club meetings.

Each August the Marion Lions Club sponsored "Old Folks Day," which annually attracted several thousand persons to the city's Matter Park. Junior society members labored to create maps, charts, illustrations, and a balsa wood replica of downtown Marion that brought back many memories to those who had watched Marion develop. One major exhibit was an oversized map of Grant County that showed the location of many points of historical interest. A legend explaining each location bordered the map. Flashlight bulbs, powered by a phonograph turntable, paired lights at each location with the corresponding explanation and remained lit long enough for the description to be read and the location determined before moving on to the next pair.

Other major civic activities continued. The juniors seized the opportunity to place historical markers throughout Grant County and conducted a successful community-wide fund drive to mark forty locations. Created by unemployed artists through the Federal Works Progress Administration, they were designed to last only a few years, yet at least two still stand more than sixty years later.

Seeing the need for a concise Grant County history book, the juniors wrote, edited, and published an updated version titled *A Century of Development: Grant County, Indiana*. Community interest was unexpectedly great, and the publication sold out quickly, leaving demand unsatisfied.

While the many civic activities were going on, the juniors arranged a series of speakers on historical subjects for the Marion High School daily convocations. As the crown jewel of the offerings, the Society sponsored an appearance by retired United States Supreme Court justice Willis Van Devanter, a Marion native and a twenty-six-year member of the Court, who returned occasionally.

Imagine the thrill of the two members who called for the justice at his hotel and their amazement when he arrived at the high school, extinguished his cigar, and placed it on the car floor.

"That will be all right, boys," he said. "I'll finish smoking it when I get back."

Wishing to share the opportunities offered by broader community service, the Marion club sponsored a student-teacher convention in Marion to explore the possibility of forming a statewide organization. The seventy teachers and students, who represented twenty schools, endorsed the proposal enthusiastically, and the Indiana Junior

Historical Society, with strong support from the Indiana
Historical Society and Governor Henry F. Schricker, was
born.

Richard S. Simons
Marion

Preface

Recording the story of the first sixty years of the Indiana Junior Historical Society was a fascinating, if intermittent, undertaking. For nearly a decade, the task involved two writers and several staff members of the Indiana Historical Society and the Indiana Historical Bureau. We dug through records, squinted at old photographs, pieced together timelines, interviewed participants, and tried to pin down facts with sometimes skimpy documentation.

The members and sponsors of the junior society richly deserved a full account that did justice to their achievements. We hope their patience has been rewarded. Narrating the adventures of "the juniors" was a chance to be amazed, many times, by the dedication and creativity that have carried this group through six decades of changing memberships, management, and education standards.

As junior historians in Indiana found new ways to reinterpret and understand their ancestors, they became an institution, a solid statewide federation of school clubs supported by a professional and energetic central office. The Indiana Junior Historical Society has few peers, and we hope that the new century will again see other young historians turning to their Hoosier counterparts for advice on creating an organization with staying power.

Junior historians will also find a host of adults who have been enormously helpful to the group and this history. Numerous people have provided assistance, and their efforts are deeply appreciated. Special thanks are due to Pamela Bennett and Dani Pfaff at the Indiana Historical Bureau, and Thomas A. Mason, Robert M. Taylor, Jr., Paula Corpuz, Shirley McCord, Kathy Breen, George Hanlin, Thomas K. Krasean, Nancy Wolfe, and Patricia Gillogly of the Indiana Historical Society.

Junior historians rarely outgrow their interest in the past. It just gets more compelling. Whether they are taking their children to Civil War battlefields or studying genealogy, they continue to make connections between yesterday and tomorrow.

The life of Richard S. Simons, one of the founders of the Indiana Junior Historical Society in 1938 and a trustee emeritus of the Indiana Historical Society, is illustrative. In 1998 he received the George W. and Constance M. Hilton Book Award from the Railway and Locomotive Historical Society for *Railroads of Indiana,* which he wrote with Francis H. Parker and published with Indiana University Press in 1997. The book is the first-ever overall history and reference on Indiana railroads from 1838 to the present.

The authors salute Mr. Simons not only for his award-winning book and lifelong passion for history, but also for building an enduring organization with historians of several generations.

January 1999

CHAPTER 1

Pioneers to the Past

They have left traces of themselves across Indiana.

In 1974 members of the Indiana Junior Historical Society helped restore the Goddard School in Homer, which was built in 1885 and used until 1916. Junior historians laid new flooring, revarnished the wainscoting, painted the walls and exterior trim, and dedicated the rejuvenated building in 1974.[1]

In the early 1980s in Flora, the Carroll County Junior-Senior Historians repaired a log cabin and are furnishing it with furniture created between the 1830s and the 1880s, when Hoosiers would have lived in similar structures. Each December the Carroll Historians reenact a log cabin Christmas celebration from a specific year for the community.[2]

Over in Modoc the Union Little Hoosiers moved a log house in 1995 to land behind Union Elementary School on State Road 36. The students corresponded with the granddaughters of previous owners to learn more about life in the primitive farm dwelling, which will be restored.

Junior historians in the 1960s and 1970s compiled a collection of award-winning architectural surveys, including studies of Rush County, Vernon, Oldenburg, churches in Cass County, schoolhouses in Posey County, and farm buildings around the state. Another team of juniors contributed to the Indiana Historical Bureau's 1966 *Directory of Historical Markers,* published to commemorate the state's sesquicentennial.

Beginning in 1990 the Hayden Little Hoosiers helped convert former governor Edgar Whitcomb's chicken coop into the Hayden Historical Museum, which by 1996 included a meeting room, a library of some five hundred volumes, and a collection of donated materials from Whitcomb's life and political career.[3]

Other teams of juniors helped delineate the boundaries of old Fort Knox II near Vincennes in 1970 and the "finest poultry house in Jefferson County" at Madison's Lanier Mansion in 1993.[4]

In Henry County juniors cleaned up Current Cemetery, which dates back to the 1840s. In this 1995 project, one of many cemetery cleanups and searches, the students cut down overgrown brush, reset fallen markers, and replaced footstones, making the cemetery visible from the road for the first time in many years.[5]

Members of the Indiana Junior Historical Society have not always left physical evidence of their activities. Sometimes they just listened, and other times they went to summer camps to master bygone skills with tools of another era and learn the legends, dances, and songs of the earliest Hoosiers. On canoe trips, by bus, and in caravans they have retraced historical routes, interviewed old-timers for oral history projects, and toured the homes, farms, and businesses of pioneer Hoosiers.

Since 1938 members of the Indiana Junior Historical Society have made history as they studied it, reenacted it, and preserved it. The surviving original members are now well within the realm of retirement, but they created a network of local history clubs that lasted from World War II to the World Wide Web. The current members clearly expect to be poking into records, unearthing treasures, and breathing new life into old buildings and stories into the next century. Only a handful of other states can claim such an enduring group of curious time travelers.

Kevin Stonerock, who grew up in the Knightstown High School History Club and served as director of the IJHS from 1987 to 1989, recalled his experiences:

> I have chicken danced; paddled a canoe until I was sure my arms would break; walked backwards off a cliff (with rope attached); slept in tents and Holiday Inns; been attacked by Indians, Confederate soldiers, and wild animals. I have painted, sawed, hammered, whittled, drilled, and scraped. I've been measured for a coffin, burned by

a bow drill, chased by a dog, and strung up over a fire pit. And all in the name of history.[6]

Not every junior has had Stonerock's colorful inclinations, but most have discovered important facts about their communities, their ancestors, and themselves in their history clubs and in state activities.

At the 1996 IJr.HS Annual Convention, which took place that year at Randolph County Junior-Senior High School in Lynn, Indiana, a foursome from Carroll County Junior High presented the compelling stories of four real-life characters from World War II. Steve Catron played his grandfather, George B. Catron, an army veteran who served in the Pacific Theater. Abby McConnell portrayed Rosalie Brown, better known as Rosie the Riveter. Dana Marcellino played Anne Noggle, a member of the Women's Army Corps, and Christopher Moore played Libero Puccini, an Italian POW who was held at Camp Atterbury from 1943 to 1945.[7]

These four students worked for weeks on their program called "The War Is Over" and spent hours at the convention describing, among other things, Catron's multiple duties as a medic, electrician, tail gunner, and pilot, and how Puccini found his way back to the United States and his bride-to-be in Ohio after the war. The students' banter and eagerness to act out the stories revealed considerable knowledge and a zeal to share it. For their efforts they won second place in the interpretive exhibits competition for the junior-senior division that day.[8] Each credited Glen Dillman, adviser of the school's history group, The Sycamore Club, with sparking his or her interest in the past.

In 1974, Jon Turpin, then seventeen, helped restore the Goddard School near Homer. Turpin, who lived in Greensboro, was president of the Junior Historical Society that year.
The Indianapolis Star and News

Carroll County Historians log cabin Christmas Celebration, 1994. *Glen Dillman*

(Top) Moving day was 15 September 1995 for the log house in Modoc. It was moved from Glen and Mary Wolfe's property to Union Elementary School. *Indiana Historical Bureau*

(Bottom) Rodger Ruddick and some of the Hayden Little Hoosiers who transformed Governor Edgar Whitcomb's chicken coop into a museum. *Indiana Historical Bureau*

A work party of junior historians at the site of Fort Knox II in 1970. *Indiana Historical Bureau*

Dillman realized in fifth grade that he wanted to be a history teacher, and, at the end of thirty years in the classroom (often disguised as a historical figure), he cannot imagine retiring. Dillman believes that "kids will respond to a challenge if you tantalize them." He must be on to something. Among hundreds of other adventures, the "1984 Indiana Teacher of the Year" has helped students restore the 1831 Adams Mill near Cutler, build a scale model of the mill and donate it to the Carroll County Museum, simulate a body snatching, and discover previously unknown records that cleared up a mystery surrounding the Carroll County Bell.[9]

There is something special about a guy who has spent six months sleeping on a World War I army cot in a modified quail hatchery at Muscatatuck Park in Jennings County —just so he could teach blacksmithing, portray a character, or otherwise lead youngsters to enjoy history at the juniors' summer camps.

Dillman represents the dedication of a long line of history club sponsors in Indiana who have inspired and sustained local groups and worked for the statewide organization since its beginning in 1938. "The sponsors are the key to everything we do," confirmed Nancy Wolfe, director of the junior society since 1991 and a sponsor in the Warsaw Community School Corporation from 1981 to 1988. One source of Wolfe's own lifelong interest in history was an early fascination with a book of Mathew Brady's Civil War photographs. "I would look for hours at that old book," she said. "I can still see the eyes of the prisoners at Andersonville."[10]

Marjorie Snodgrass, who sponsored a Little Hoosier club at Indianapolis Public School 110 from 1984 to 1989, was wistful when she recalled her group's activities, which usually took place after school. Among other projects, her students made a quilt, constructed a miniature pioneer village, and tackled a replica of the Soldiers and Sailors Monument located in downtown Indianapolis. "I just liked doing it," said Snodgrass, who often drove students home after meetings because court-ordered busing had limited their transportation options. "I looked forward to that day, and I had neat kids who wanted to stay after school. It was one of the things I missed most when I retired."[11]

Sponsors can spend unbelievable amounts of time during school, after hours, on weekends, and through the summer leading bands of juniors to archaeological digs, workshops, cemetery explorations, camping trips, bike tours, architectural studies, and all manner of interesting undertakings—and all in the name of history.

"It's kind of addicting," admitted Fred Williams, who served as director of the juniors' summer camp program from 1993 to 1997. Sponsor of the Carl J. Polk Little Hoosiers Club in Lake Station and a teacher, Williams claimed that it is simple to hold the interest of budding historians. "Just take them places and organize good speakers," he said, veering quickly into an enthusiastic description of plans for the 1996 "Indian Life" camp that included an encampment, beadwork, wood carving, games, canoeing, swimming, and leather crafts.[12]

"The sponsors' effectiveness comes from really loving history and wanting to share it," said Wolfe. "You have to be almost obsessed."[13]

Ron Woodward, sponsor of the history club at Wabash Middle School (formerly Wabash Junior High), attributed his passion for history to a wise third-grade teacher in New Albany, who helped him overcome reading difficulties by insisting that he read—a lot. "She set aside time every day for me to pick out books in the school library and read what I liked," he explained. By choice, he plowed through the state histories and delved into chronicles about the Roman Empire and the French Revolution. By seventh grade he realized he knew more than one of his social studies teachers, and his zest for the past has not waned since.[14]

The 1996 summer camp codirector Tammy Artis, a teacher at Brush Creek Elementary School in Jennings County and sponsor of the Hauser Junior-Senior High Historians in Hope, was nearing the end of her eighteenth year with the juniors, having started at age ten. Typical of many juniors, Artis maintained an interest in history—and junior society activities—long after high school graduation.[15]

"This organization has a funny way of becoming a part of you," said David Roberts when he stepped down as the juniors' state president in 1993.[16] After graduating from Wabash College, Roberts received his Indiana Teaching License for Social Studies and English in 1997. He worked for six months at Conner Prairie Museum as an apprentice woodworker and is now working on his master's at the University of North Carolina. This sponsor-in-the-making fondly recalled his experiences as a youngster at John Strange Elementary School in Indianapolis, under the tutelage of Judy Smith. "We did a parade of famous Hoosiers, a pioneer craft fair, and a three-day field trip to Lincoln's Boyhood Home," said Roberts.[17]

Perhaps the quintessential junior historian of his generation, Mike Westfall was active in the Allen County Junior Historical Society in the mid-1960s and a leader and adviser in the state movement into the 1970s. Westfall holds a master's degree in American history from the College of William and Mary in Williamsburg, Virginia, and serves on the Steering Committee of the Jamestown National Historic Site in Virginia. He was elected to the Indiana Historical Society's Board of Trustees in 1994 and chaired the Society's Building Committee for the construction of the new 165,000-square-foot, four-story headquarters. A resident of Fort Wayne, Westfall is director of property management at Parkview Memorial Hospital there.

Although he still gets his hands dirty at archaeological digs and carries out his Society responsibilities with obvious relish, Westfall has some pretty serious reasons for making history a central element of his life. "It gives you a touchstone for judging the outcome of your decisions," he said. "We were sitting on a seawall at Jamestown talking about how discouraging it can be to work with kids who have no sense of history. Until you see what's behind, you become totally focused on the immediate. History makes the future a little more predictable."[18]

Thanks to the work of Westfall and many others in the Indiana Junior Historical Society, thousands of Hoosiers have grown up with a strong sense of history.

* * * *

(Top) At summer camp in 1972, junior historians learned to dye yarn with the same roots and plants used by pioneers. *Indiana Historical Bureau*

(Bottom) Current Cemetery cleanup. *IJr.HS (IHS)*

Kevin Stonerock as Billy Yank. *IJr.HS (IHS)*

(Top) Christopher Moore, Steve Catron, Dana Marcellino, and Abby McConnell from Carroll County Junior High School presented "The War Is Over" as an interpretive exhibit at the 1996 Annual Convention. *IJr.HS (IHS)*

(Bottom, left) Glen Dillman in costume. *Indiana Historical Bureau*
(Bottom, center) Nancy Wolfe, who became director of the Indiana Junior Historical Society in 1991, was a sponsor in the Warsaw Community School Corporation from 1981 to 1988. *Indiana Historical Bureau*
(Bottom, right) Fred Williams, camp director, 1993–97. *IJr.HS (IHS)*

Indianapolis Public School 110 with its quilt display at the 1989 Annual Convention. Marjorie Snodgrass was the sponsor for the group from 1984 to 1989. *Marjorie Snodgrass scrapbook*

Historians for the Future

Together and independently, the Indiana Historical Society and the Indiana Historical Bureau, a state agency, have nurtured the junior group. Without the financial and administrative support of these two organizations, junior leaders could not have sustained their statewide network of clubs and sponsors. Other organizations, including the Society of Indiana Pioneers, the Colonial Dames, the Indiana Department of Education, as well as numerous smaller groups, made significant contributions at critical times.

Individuals who are unfamiliar with historical activities in Indiana frequently confuse the Society and the Bureau, which is natural. Both organizations are dedicated, logically enough, to Indiana's history. Both have been responsible for the development of the IJr.HS. Even their names sound alike.

In truth, they are separate entities with distinct purposes. From the 1920s until the 1970s, however, they were intertwined. Their differences were blurred as they shared office space, responsibilities, staff, and even administrators.

The Indiana Historical Bureau is a permanent agency of state government. With the Indiana State Library it makes up the Library and Historical Department, which is supervised by a board of gubernatorial appointees. The Bureau originated in 1915 as the Indiana Historical Commission, created by the General Assembly to organize the state's centennial celebration in 1916. From 1919 forward, General Assembly appropriations have supported the commission, which was renamed the Indiana Historical Bureau in 1925.

The Indiana Historical Society is a private, nonprofit membership organization established in 1830 by a group of prominent Hoosiers. In the early 1920s the Society was supported by membership fees, a small Indiana Historical Commission allocation for publications, and a modest income from the William H. English estate. Generous gifts, most notably a 1977 bequest from the estate of Eli Lilly, boosted the Society's endowment and library holdings and made the organization a powerful force in publishing and historical circles.

The Indiana Junior Historical Society developed in the context of how history and social studies have been taught in Indiana. During its first sixty years, the junior group was affected by, and even attempted to shape, policies on content and methods made by teachers and government officials. Although the organization insists on looking backward, a 1996 assessment suggests that it has always been ahead of its time. "Current state recommendations about more hands-on experiences, more curricula developed by teachers, more teamwork, more emphasis on local programs, and less reliance on textbooks are the kinds of things the juniors have always done," said Mary Fortney, social studies consultant for the Indiana Department of Education.[19]

Policies notwithstanding, junior sponsors represent the most important qualities of any teacher in any generation. They do not separate their functions as teachers and sponsors. Even the few sponsors who are not schoolteachers are making history come alive for their members, underscoring with every activity the junior society's enduring slogan: "History Is Fun!" Trends and distractions will come and go, but "kids are still eager and hungry for someone to take the time to show them things, explain events, and open their eyes," claims sponsor and teacher Ron Woodward.[20]

Although the juniors made Hoosier heritage an extracurricular option in the late 1930s, teachers had been presenting Indiana history in classrooms for more than twenty years. In 1899 the forty-sixth session of the Indiana State Teachers Association (ISTA) discussed "How Can We Interest the People and Bring about a More Thorough and Systematic and Comprehensive Study of the History of Indiana?"[21] The State and Local Historical Committee of the Indiana Department of Public Instruction, with the backing of the ISTA, recommended to the Superintendent of Public Instruction in 1899 "the introduction of Indiana history and civil government into the public schools."[22] The committee also included two definitive outlines of topics to cover and sources to use and preserve for the study of local history, with commentary excerpted below:

> Our people in this comparatively new country have not yet appreciated the value of local history and of records made "upon the spot." This is especially true in these Central States, where so much time and effort has been consumed in the merely physical aspects of life. Especially have few people of Indiana yet realized the historic value of apparently commonplace occurrences, and we must learn it soon and begin to preserve what we have of historic value or we shall soon have passed the point beyond which it will be impossible for us to collect much of our early history, which is vastly significant.[23]

Available records do not reveal immediate acceptance of the committee's recommendation, but the state's centennial celebration in 1916 sparked renewed interest. The Indiana Historical Commission, predecessor of the Bureau, "prepared a rather comprehensive outline or course of study in Indiana history for use throughout the grades, which the State Board of Education placed in its manual for teachers," wrote Harlow Lindley, commission secretary, in the official account of the centennial observance.[24] Lindley acknowledged that the extent to which Indiana history was seriously pursued "was dependent largely upon the capacity and alertness of the school authorities in the counties as well as upon the ability and fitness of teachers," but he asserted that a profound interest had been stirred.[25] "An immediate and concrete result in this awakened interest is found in the fact that the State Board of Education has already arranged for the inclusion in the United States history text-book of an adequate supplement on Indiana history," wrote Lindley. "Furthermore, the Board adopted an 'Indiana' speller, the words in which have to do with the life and environment of the State."[26]

Indiana schoolchildren had an indefatigable champion in commission member Charity Dye, who edited "The Centennial Story Hour" for the Sunday issues of the *Indianapolis Star.* In a project that paralleled many later junior activities, she coordinated a statewide letter exchange, "wherein pupils from different parts of the State wrote each other of the interesting things in the history and life of their respective neighborhoods."[27]

At a meeting in December 1919 for all state organizations interested in Indiana history, however, delegates agreed that "neither by legislative enactment, requirements

Tammy Artis taught spinning at Little Hoosier Camp. *Indiana Historical Bureau*

(Top) Ron Woodward. *IJr.HS (IHS)*

(Bottom, left) David Roberts and Judy Smith. *IJr.HS (IHS)*
(Bottom, right) Mike Westfall. *IHS*

Charity Dye. *IHS*

The Indiana Historical Commission shown in this 1916 photograph planned the celebration of the centennial of statehood in 1916 and was the genesis of the Indiana Historical Bureau. (Front row, left to right: Samuel M. Foster, Frank B. Wynn, Governor Samuel M. Ralston, Charles W. Moores, James A. Woodburn; back row: Lew O'Bannon, John Cavanaugh, Harlow Lindley, Charity Dye.)
Indiana State Library

of the State Board of Education, nor the requirements of local school authorities had any steps been taken for the systematic teaching of state and local history."[28] In January 1920 a special committee from that meeting presented the following recommendations to the State Board of Education, which unanimously adopted them in February 1920:

1. That the time devoted to history in the eighth grade be divided between United States history, Indiana history, and local history, provided that the time given to Indiana history shall include a study of the civil government of the state.

2. That as a means of placing information in the hands of teachers and students, the special chapter feature now in the adopted text book on United States history (which special chapter is devoted entirely to Indiana history) be and the same is hereby ordered continued in the next text book adopted; provided, however, that said special chapter shall contain a bibliography of Indiana history of not less than thirty titles.

3. That for the school year of 1920 and 1921 and annually thereafter, the State Superintendent of Public Instruction *shall* furnish an outline of the special chapter on Indiana history now in the adopted U.S. History text to all teachers of the eighth grade and the said outline *shall* furnish and be the basis for teaching Indiana history in the schools of the state.

4. That after January 1, 1921, and annually thereafter the State Superintendent of Public Instruction *shall*

furnish questions to all persons who wish to be graduated from the common schools of the state and that a satisfactory examination in Indiana history *shall* constitute a condition for the promotion of any pupil from the eighth grade to any higher school in the state. Also, that a record of a satisfactory examination in Indiana history shall be entered on the diploma or certificate of graduation of each pupil who graduates from the eighth grade.[29]

Reporting at the 1924 annual Indiana History Conference, Professor Herbert Briggs of Terre Haute, who had chaired the committee, admonished: "May we hope that the conditions have entirely passed when we will waste time in discussing the *wisdom* of teaching our state history in the schools of the state!"[30]

Between the centennial and 1938, a series of educators and teenagers attempted to coordinate a statewide extracurricular junior historical movement. As early as 1922 Oscar H. Williams, then supervisor of teacher training in the Department of Public Instruction, drew up a plan of voluntary junior historical societies in the upper six years of school. His plan even included publication of a junior magazine of history.[31] John W. Oliver, assistant director of the Indiana Historical Commission, approved the idea, as did the Indiana Historical Society, but no such organization emerged.[32]

Although students founded a number of independent history clubs, many of the organizations were short-lived. Williams applauded the creation of the New Albany Junior

Historical Society and Nature Study Club and another club in Tipton:

> In junior historical societies are found the means of making concrete applications of many truths learned in American history, and of using the criteria for judging the validity of historical evidence. For presenting vivid and colorful experiences of people on a level, easily understood and interpreted by children, for first-hand sensory data of historical materials . . . nothing can surpass the work, if properly organized and directed, of the junior historical societies.[33]

In a list of potential projects for young historians, Williams included archaeological surveys, historical marker research, and local history studies.[34]

For all the merit of the individual club activities, however, no one in the 1920s or early 1930s could coordinate a statewide organization. The Indiana Historical Society formed a High School Committee in 1931 to be a clearinghouse for junior clubs and teachers of Indiana history.[35] Educators and students continued to express interest in a statewide network, but the junior history movement, "if it can be called such, was exceedingly sporadic," said Christopher B. Coleman in 1941.[36] Coleman was a longtime official of the Bureau, Society, and Indiana State Library.

Two members of the Grant County Junior Historical Society finally succeeded in creating a lasting organization in 1938. Richard S. Simons and William Sell received the support of the executive committee of the Indiana Historical Society in late 1937 to look into the creation of a statewide network of junior history groups.[37]

The Grant County group had been innovative since its establishment in 1936. Club members spoke at gatherings, compiled historical data, raised money for forty markers for historic sites, and prepared exhibits and distributed three thousand Old Northwest Territory maps for the annual Old Folks' Day. The club also organized a "Local History Week" during which the club sponsored speakers, wrote newspaper articles, and cooperated with downtown merchants. One of the club's most successful efforts was the publication of *A Century of Development: Grant County, Indiana* in April 1937. Members sold more than 950 copies.[38]

With authorization from the Indiana Historical Society, members of the Grant County group invited schools from all over the state to send representatives to the Indiana Teacher-Student History Convention at Marion High School on 9 April 1938.[39] Although it is not clear how many invitations were sent, state records indicate that there were 83 senior high schools, 37 junior high schools, 49 junior-senior high schools, and 679 combined elementary-high schools operating in Indiana at that time.[40]

More than seventy persons attended the 1938 conference representing twenty schools, seven of which had sponsored history clubs.[41] The Grant County Junior Historical Society and the history club of Shortridge High School in Indianapolis set up an exhibit of Indian relics, paintings, maps, historical society publications, and student compositions.[42]

(Top) Christopher B. Coleman. *IHS*

(Bottom) Richard S. Simons. *IHS*

The IJHS spring convention of 1944 was held on the historic campus of Arsenal Technical High School in Indianapolis. The federal government built an arsenal on the site between 1863 and 1893, and the army occupied the facility until 1903. The high school opened in 1912. *Hester Anne Hale*

The day was filled with speeches and a roundtable discussion about the formation of history and social science clubs in the state. Historian Ross Franklin Lockridge of Bloomington accompanied the delegates on a tour along the Frances Slocum Trail. At the nearby Mississinewa Battleground, Lockridge described the last Indian battle east of the Mississippi River. At the evening campfire he talked of Frances Slocum's life.

The conference generated enthusiasm for a junior history organization. Meeting in July and November 1938, members of the Indiana Historical Society's executive committee decided against junior memberships in the adult group, preferring to promote high school or junior county historical societies. Committee members agreed to contribute up to ten dollars for the group's establishment and a state meeting of its representatives in 1939.[43] At the Indiana History Conference in Indianapolis in December 1938, the Society membership voted to establish a permanent junior historical organization.[44]

In promoting the new group, Richard Simons said, "From the beginning we have endeavored to keep one fact constantly before us; that this is an historical society and not a school room history class. We feel that we must learn the history of our community through live, worthwhile projects and not through mass study of some text. Research, of course, is essential and plays some part in our activities, but it is not the most important point in our program."[45]

Horace Bailey Carroll, the Texas historian who founded a junior group in the Lone Star State in 1940, recognized the Hoosiers' pioneering role in the movement. "The initial development of the idea was, to the best of my knowledge, in Indiana," he said.[46] Carroll's eloquent endorsement of the junior historians mirrored the drive of kindred spirits in Indiana: "The whole force of the movement is directed toward developing a greater knowledge of one's homeland. The importance of this arises from the fact that in an orderly succession, this knowledge is a prerequisite to a love of homeland, which in its turn is the basic essential of any worth while patriotism."[47] The May 1940 issue of the *Indiana History Bulletin* took note of the young and eager sister group in Texas.

Seven high schools were represented at the December 1938 Indiana Historical Society meeting: Marion, Hartford City, Fort Wayne Central, and Lafayette Jefferson, and from Indianapolis, Shortridge, George Washington, and Arsenal Technical. Fred Jones of Shortridge High School was named temporary president and Virginia Washburn of Arsenal Technical, temporary secretary-treasurer. As sponsor, the Indiana Historical Society noted that the new organization had "plans to develop activities similar to those of the Junior Academy of Science."[48] Students scheduled another general meeting for the spring, and the Grant County club agreed to draft a constitution and present it at the spring meeting for revision and adoption.

The juniors' first annual conference took place in April 1939 at Shortridge High School in Indianapolis. More than one hundred persons represented eleven high schools: Bloomington's University High School, Goshen, Hartford

City, Marion, Vincennes, and Waynetown, and Arsenal Technical, Howe, Washington, Broad Ripple, and Shortridge of Indianapolis. Delegates elected John D. Williams of Arsenal Technical as the first president.[49]

The junior society, continuing the tradition of a spring meeting, convened on 13 April 1940 in Bloomington with the Cliocrat Club of University High School as host. Approximately two hundred delegates were treated to a welcome from Indiana University president Herman B Wells and talks on New Harmony's restoration, changing concepts of patriotism, and current history in Europe, which was already at war.

Delegates adopted a permanent constitution providing for a president; two vice presidents, one from northern Indiana and one from southern Indiana; a secretary-treasurer; and an executive committee consisting of the officers and three other members elected by the membership. Officers elected in 1940 included Henrietta Parrish of Bloomington as president, Walter Dunn of Indianapolis as vice president, north, William Dau of Aurora as vice president, south, and Marjorie Norman of Marion as secretary-treasurer.[50]

The president, with the approval of the executive committee, was to select a junior and a senior adviser "from among those persons who are particularly experienced in the work and the undertakings of the society."[51] Coleman became the first senior adviser and Simons the first junior adviser of the IJHS.[52]

In early 1939 the Society named Simons chairman of the Committee on Junior Historical Organizations.[53] Simons and Coleman provided a link between the Bureau and the Society in Indianapolis and the clubs around the state. However, no single individual at either the Bureau or the Society had specific responsibility for managing or promoting the IJHS.

Early leaders apparently expected little more from the IJHS than a meeting in conjunction with the Society's annual conference in December and the convention of junior clubs each spring. Representatives of the IJHS became regular participants in the December Indiana History Conference.[54]

Then, as now, the success of the IJHS depended on the schools' social studies teachers who served as club sponsors. As long as the clubs were involved in activities relating to local and state history, the IJHS had a reason to gather twice a year.

For the spring convention of 1941, the Social Studies Club of Arsenal Technical High School invited members to its historic campus. Fourteen schools sent 189 individuals. Nine of these schools were IJHS members: Arsenal Technical, Shortridge, Warren Central, University High School, Aurora, Goshen, Hartford City, Marion, and New Castle.[55] George Washington High School's club was also a member but through an error was not listed.[56] For the first time, only member clubs were permitted to vote on convention business.

The Arsenal Technical club "made unusually attractive arrangements for the program and for entertainment of the visitors" and attracted a "generous amount of publicity" from the newspapers.[57] Harry O. Garmon, a civil engineer and amateur historian, spoke about "Pioneer Indiana History as a Hobby," and William H. Remy, the Marion County prosecutor in the 1920s who successfully convicted Ku Klux Klansman D. C. Stephenson, discussed "The Tradition of Freedom as Reflected in American Literature."[58]

Although the Bureau offered the juniors space in the *Indiana History Bulletin,* in the fall of 1941 the junior society began publishing its own monthly newsletter, the *Bulletin: Indiana Junior Historical Society,* edited by the state president, Edward McKinney, Jr., of Arsenal Technical. Three issues appeared from October through December 1941. In January 1942 students changed the title to *The Junior Historian;* and in February, March, and May to *Junior History Bulletin.*[59] When a junior delegate in 1942 questioned the newsletter's value and suggested that the Bureau's *Indiana History Bulletin* was sufficient, other delegates backed the continued production of a separate publication.[60]

In October 1941 the young historians spoke confidently of the future: "Although the annual meeting and annual convention of the society are highlights of the year's activities, plans are being advanced to include other activities for both the individual societies and clubs and for the state society as a whole."[61] The IJHS, however, could not avoid the effects of American involvement in World War II.

CHAPTER 2

Retreat and Revival: The War Years

The 1942 spring convention of the Indiana Junior Historical Society, which took place in Aurora in southeastern Indiana, was well attended considering the distance for northern Indiana schools and the wartime restrictions on automobile travel. The delegates visited the grave site of President William Henry Harrison at North Bend, Ohio.[1] Existing records list only seven member clubs in 1942: Aurora, Hartford City, New Castle, Marion, Milan, Dillsboro, and Arsenal Technical.[2] The nominating committee at the Aurora convention realized its goal of placing a representative of every member school in an office.[3]

In 1942 outgoing president Edward McKinney, Jr., felt that the IJHS probably was facing its most fateful year. The convention, which had been the chief link between clubs, was facing cancellation due to gas rationing, and, as a result, members might need to conduct officer elections through the newsletter. In the light of such obstacles, Otho Winger of North Manchester stressed taking an interest in the community and supporting local boys serving in the armed forces.[4]

The war affected individual clubs in numerous ways. The draft age was lowered to eighteen in June 1942, and those as young as seventeen were encouraged to volunteer. Some teachers were called into the armed services, and many students took part-time jobs after school and on Saturdays.[5] Extracurricular activities focused on scrap metal drives, knitting and sewing for the Red Cross, and collecting books and magazines for servicemen.[6] Limited gasoline and restrictions on tires curtailed travel.

Attendance was small at the 1942 and 1943 IJHS gatherings, but enthusiasm was "unabated."[7] The number of reservations dropped for the May 1943 convention at Warren Central High School in Indianapolis. Only forty-two delegates were present, mainly representing schools in Marion County. Louise Ross, teacher-sponsor of the George Washington High School club, was credited with fostering much of the activity of the state group in 1943.[8]

Christopher Coleman spoke to the IJHS again at Warren Central in the spring of 1944. More than fifty persons attended the convention, but, once again, only Marion

County high schools were represented. Continuing travel difficulties limited the number of IJHS participants in the Indiana Historical Society's December 1944 history conference to officers only.[9] The 1945 IJHS spring convention was canceled. "The war has played havoc with the Junior Historical Society units," commented a writer for the Warren Central club in April 1945, who also mentioned plans for broadening the junior programs after the war.[10] The IJHS could claim only four clubs in 1945: Warren Central History Club, Shortridge High School History Club, Social Science Club of Arsenal Technical High School, and John Strange School History Club.[11]

In early December 1945 Howard H. Peckham, Coleman's successor at the Society and Bureau, initiated a meeting with thirty-seven students and teachers from seven high schools during the twenty-seventh annual Indiana History Conference. The IJHS had not met for more than a year; therefore there were no officers.

Paul Seehausen presided at the meeting. Formerly a Shortridge history club sponsor, he was a consultant at the Department of Public Instruction in 1945, giving the juniors an official link to policy makers. Seehausen emphasized the value of high school history clubs for communities and for future Indiana Historical Society membership. He believed the junior society should also include high school social science clubs focused on current events or international relations. "It was generally agreed that they all should be made to feel welcome in the Junior Historical Society," according to the January 1946 issue of the *Indiana History Bulletin*.[12]

Rather than attempt an immediate reorganization in late 1945, meeting participants decided to elect IJHS officers and reorganize at a state convention of history clubs in spring 1946. A committee composed of Seehausen, Richard S. Simons, Howard Peckham, Arsenal Technical sponsor Mary Elizabeth Moore, and Warren Central sponsor Fred Pierpont wrote to all history teachers in the state to stimulate interest in new clubs. The committee furnished a sample constitution and suggested activities and projects requiring neither textbook nor writing.[13]

Progress was slow. Apparently not enough interest developed to hold a reorganization meeting in 1946. No state officers were elected for 1946–47 or for 1947–48. Only the Anthony Wayne Club at Fort Wayne Central, organized in 1945, appeared to be active. That club received the Certificate of Award as the most active high school history club during the 1946–47 school year.[14]

Trying again to build some enthusiasm, early in 1947 Peckham organized a contest among clubs. "The time is approaching," he wrote Simons, "when I shall ask the secretaries of the various high school history clubs to report on their activities and projects during the year."[15] Responses were disappointing. From Beech Grove, Broad Ripple, Warren Central, and Wolcott came reports of very little activity during 1947–48. Arsenal Technical, Shortridge, and Washington had conducted only a few meetings. Warsaw High School made no report, but Peckham was not deterred. "I think we should get the competition started at all costs, and say little about the lack of competition," he said.[16]

Howard Peckham with the officers and sponsors of the Indiana Junior Historical Society in 1950. In addition to reviving the IJHS after World War II, Peckham opened the membership of the Indiana Historical Society to the public, built the collections of the William Henry Smith Library, and supervised the production of many outstanding publications and leaflets for Indiana schoolchildren. *IHS*

Hubert Hawkins and Gayle Thornbrough. *IHS*

The Indiana Historical Society's Committee on Junior Historical Organizations reported in 1948 that it was again cooperating with the Bureau to find the state's most active high school club to receive a Certificate of Award. The committee observed that the contest was being held in 1948 "with more hope than confidence."[17]

Persistent committee efforts, especially from the three members based in Indianapolis—Simons, Seehausen, and Gayle Thornbrough, then an editor for the Indiana Historical Bureau—finally paid off in 1949. In January 1949 the Department of Public Instruction sent a questionnaire "To certain High School Principals and heads of Senior High School Social Studies Departments." It explained that while the IJHS's primary interest was state and local history, it was "eager to enlist in its membership such High School organizations as are willing to devote some part of their activities to this field."[18]

In late March 1949 Seehausen sent a letter to principals announcing two regional conferences to discuss the junior organization. School clubs south of US 40 east of Indianapolis and US 36 to the west convened 23 April at Spring Mill State Park while clubs north of the line met in Monticello one week later.[19]

Twelve high schools were represented at the Monticello meeting (Morocco, East Chicago Washington, Lebanon, Fort Wayne Central, Medaryville, Hammond, Tipton, Fortville, Anderson, Speedway, La Porte, and Monticello) and seven at Spring Mill (Columbus, Mitchell, Decker, Terre Haute Gerstmeyer, Decatur Township of Marion County, Bedford, and Beech Grove).[20] More than 130 students and teachers participated. The two state meetings were almost identical, with Ross Franklin Lockridge of Indiana University as the featured speaker. At both meetings delegates heard a musical program by high school students and watched a film, *Indiana Has Almost Everything.* Each began with informal sightseeing and concluded with a social period.

The most important result of the 1949 conferences was the recommitment of the high school clubs to the Indiana Junior Historical Society. Each school in attendance named a student representative to an executive committee.[21] The Bureau announced that it would begin publishing a monthly newsletter, the *Hoosier Historian,* in the fall of 1949. The IJHS decided to continue presenting a special award every spring to the year's most active club.

In May 1949 the Indiana University Foundation announced that it would award scholarships of one hundred dollars each to two senior students, one in the northern half of the state and one in the southern half, for prizewinning essays.[22] The 1949 essay competition topics reflected the broadening of the school clubs' interests. For students in clubs involved in Indiana history, the subject was "The Significance of 150 Years of Transportation Development in Indiana."[23] For current events and international relations clubs, the subject was modern transportation and communications in a shrinking world. Both topics were linked to the sesquicentennial observance of Indiana's establishment as a territory in 1800.[24]

The IJHS executive committee met in October 1949 in Indianapolis.[25] Members voted to follow the IJHS's original constitution and elect state officers every spring. The committee decided to revive the IJHS meeting at the December Indiana History Conference and to support the idea of a speakers bureau.

Executive committee members expressed great interest in offering a printed charter, suitable for framing, to each IJHS chapter. Charters, which became available in November 1949, were issued on behalf of the Bureau, the Society, and the Department of Public Instruction. Also at the October meeting the executive committee took action on the design of a pin for IJHS members.

Consistent records were not kept of the number of member clubs in the IJHS at any given time before the 1960s. As Christopher Coleman observed some years earlier, some high school history clubs were more active than others, and some were more durable. The peak number of member clubs for the pre–World War II years is estimated at fourteen; there may have been as many as twenty-two late in 1948. The newly elected officers, meeting in executive session on 6 May 1950, voted to charge one dollar dues per year for each chartered club. After state dues were assessed, a more precise number of active member clubs could be determined. The Bureau's 1948–50 biennial report indicated that there were seventeen active high school clubs.[26] At that time there were 165 secondary schools and 633 combined elementary and secondary schools in the state.[27]

The publication of the *Hoosier Historian* was not always predictable. Peckham was directing both the Bureau and the Society with limited funds and a small staff, and no one was charged specifically with overseeing the IJHS. In May 1950, the end of the first year of the juniors' publication,

Peckham offered continued Bureau financing for the newsletter but asked the IJHS executive board to "assume or assign" the chief responsibility for the newsletter.[28] At an IJHS executive meeting on 6 May 1950, officers voted to add editorial responsibility for the *Hoosier Historian* to the secretary's duties and make the secretary's club responsible for the publication. Marilyn Loomis, the incoming secretary-treasurer, and her club at Arsenal Technical accepted the new responsibilities.[29]

Even with limited resources, Peckham was determined to bolster the activities of school clubs and the resurgent student organization. He told Richard Simons, who was by then contributing regularly to the *Indianapolis Star Magazine*:

> In the Indiana Junior Historical Society high school students learn that history means much more than reading textbooks and memorizing dates. Club members discover their heritage by visiting historic sites and museums, by project work and research, and by programs at social gatherings. In short, they learn that history can be fun.
>
> We hope that this explanation of the past will make these young people aware of the continuity of history—that what happened yesterday affects what can and does happen today. A more intelligent and responsible citizenry is the goal.[30]

To carry out his commitment, Peckham needed an assistant to visit high schools. "We started off this past fall with seventeen active clubs," he wrote to Wilbur Young, superintendent of public instruction, on 15 January 1951. "However it now appears that many of our most enthusiastic members were graduated last June. Interest is dwindling and we can't seem to get new clubs formed in other high schools. . . . What we have always needed is a field agent who could visit the high schools, talk enthusiastically about history, and call an organizational meeting."[31]

Peckham sought Young's assistance in finding a part-time field agent. "We have great hopes for next year because of a bill in the legislature to add a man to the State Department of Instruction," Peckham wrote to an IJHS club sponsor. "I have talked to the new incoming superintendent about assigning someone to serve as field agent for the junior historical society movement, and he says we can use this new man, who will have charge of a division of adult education."[32]

Peckham put Richard Haupt on the Bureau payroll as the first field representative for the IJHS, effective 1 September 1951. As a senior history major from Hanover College, Haupt had attended an Indiana History Workshop sponsored by the Indiana State Library, the Bureau, and the Indiana Department of Conservation from 8 to 11 April 1951 at Spring Mill State Park. He met Gayle Thornbrough and Peckham, who soon offered him a part-time job "to stimulate the Indiana Junior Historical Society and the county historical societies."[33]

While studying for a master's degree in history at Indiana University, Haupt traveled on behalf of the Bureau two days per week from 1 September to 1 June. In addition to visiting schools throughout the state, Haupt was expected to serve county historical societies as an organizer, speaker, and singer. Known as the "Troubadour of Monroe County,"

Haupt later recalled driving some fifty thousand miles in his 1939 Pontiac, visiting every county in the state and most of the towns of any size.[34]

Peckham thought Haupt should be able to visit three schools each day, if only to make an appointment for a later visit. Both the Bureau director and Simons, then chairman of the Society's advisory committee to the IJHS, believed that only by growing could the junior organization last. "If it does not catch on," Peckham wrote Haupt in early 1952, "I am not sure we will continue our efforts for the benefit of only 16 or 17 clubs."[35]

Haupt reported early in 1952 that seemingly interested faculty sponsors and students failed to establish school clubs after his visits. He asked for something specific to leave with them—charters, membership cards, copies of the *Hoosier Historian*—anything that would obligate the schools to make commitments to the IJHS.[36] Gradually, the number of member schools increased. By June 1953, the end of Haupt's two-year stint with the IJHS, twenty clubs were active members, although to that time approximately thirty high school clubs had been chartered.[37]

The IJHS reestablished its spring conference in 1953 after much discussion about the advantages of regional meetings versus large statewide meetings. Also leaders considered reinstituting certain recognition awards. In May, eleven high schools sent 125 students to the IJHS spring conference in Bloomington. Professor Stephen G. Savage made a presentation about steamboating on the Ohio River, and delegates visited the university library to see rare materials on Lincoln and unusual books on the Far West.[38]

The Indiana University Foundation scholarship competition had not attracted the response it expected. No entries were submitted from the northern region in 1950, but Mary Alice Patton of Columbus High School won for the southern region.[39] Marilyn Loomis from Arsenal Technical won for the northern region in 1951, a year in which no one competed from the southern region.[40] After 1952, when Kathryn Arbuckle of Morocco High School and Jane Reeder of Columbus High School were awarded scholarships, there are no further records of competition winners.[41] Peckham believed the essay competition had helped "to enliven and enlarge" the junior society.[42]

Junior leaders continued to recognize the most active history club each year and in 1952 changed the award from a certificate to a trophy. The Lebanon High School club was the first to win the trophy, with the Bureau noting that it was "especially impressed by its project for studying county history."[43] Also inscribed on the metal plate of the new trophy were the names of previous winners for the most active club: the Anthony Wayne Club of Fort Wayne Central (1949), the Pierian Club of Columbus (1950), and the Decatur Central History Club (1951).[44]

Another change came about with the appointment of Hubert H. Hawkins to serve as director of the Bureau and executive secretary of the Society in 1953. At the beginning of his tenure Hawkins was on his own with the IJHS. After Haupt's departure in mid-1953, the Bureau had no replacement "and no money for one, either."[45] Haupt had no successor until Joseph Martin, a Korean War veteran studying history at Butler University, was hired 1 December

1954. Hawkins believed the absence of a field representative during the 1953–54 school year damaged the junior program.[46]

At the IJHS meeting in December, Martin presented a set of plans to be initiated by the spring convention. The foremost need was to build new clubs throughout the state.[47] Martin worked for a year or so, but Hawkins believed that using college students to promote the IJHS program had disadvantages. The arrangements were temporary, and academic responsibilities restricted the part-time field agents. A member of the Indiana Library and Historical Board suggested hiring a retired history teacher.[48]

DePauw University professor Herbert Heller, a former club sponsor and member of the Indiana Historical Society's School Committee from 1951 to 1956, recruited Carl Zenor to the Bureau to work for the IJHS in September 1956. Formerly a teacher and history club sponsor at Bainbridge, Zenor was teaching at George Washington High School in Indianapolis, where he had reactivated a history club. Zenor visited schools on weekends and during vacations, trying to bring new clubs into the state organization.[49]

Even with Zenor on board, the Bureau was able to hire Ronald L. Kuykendall, a graduate student at Indiana State University, in November 1959 to call on schools.[50] Kuykendall sent Zenor target lists of the schools he wanted to contact, and Zenor sent out letters of introduction and also visited schools when possible.

There were fewer than twenty IJHS member clubs in the 1959–60 school year. Even though that number was an increase over the year before, the junior movement in

Hubert Hawkins had a direct influence on the development of the IJHS from 1953 to 1976. Although he was hired as Bureau director by the Indiana Library and Historical Board and presented to the Society for the position of executive secretary, he believed the two organizations needed to maintain separate identities. *IHS*

IJHS pin. *IHS*

Indiana was static.[51] All too often the gain of a new club was offset by the loss of another. Some of the clubs avidly competed with other clubs and sent delegations to every convention; others did not even send delegates. The success and longevity of any club still depended a great deal on its sponsor.

The General Assembly continued to reject the Bureau's request for a full-time salaried IJHS director. With the money available, the best the Bureau and the Society could do was hire part-time agents. The results reflected the lack of money and field time to develop the program. Despite their dedication, Hawkins and his assistants were unable to achieve any appreciable growth in the IJHS through the 1950s.

This experience paralleled that of the Indiana Historical Society a century before. The juniors' patron group did not flourish in its early years because its leaders were busy with other causes. By the late 1870s Society officials knew they needed "someone willing to make the Society his special labor."[52] Similarly, leaders of the late 1950s and early 1960s were convinced that the junior organization would grow in size and significance only with the appointment of a full-time staff director.

One can speculate that another reason the IJHS did not grow in the 1950s was that educators in the state were preoccupied with proposals destined to streamline Indiana's school corporations and upgrade the social studies curriculum. The result was the 1959 School District Reorganization Act, which was the first legislation to affect all school districts in the state since 1852, when the General Assembly abolished thousands of school districts as administrative units and created school corporations in 935 townships and 82 cities and towns.[53] In 1873 an Office of County Superintendent had been established in each county, with provisions for the township trustees and chairmen of city school boards to elect the superintendent.

The move away from one-room schools necessitated the creation of even larger attendance areas; however, voluntary reorganization of rural township and small-town schools was not widespread in the first half of the twentieth century. As of 1956 the General Assembly had failed to establish new minimum standards for the size of school corporations. Efforts to pass a comprehensive reorganization statute failed in 1957.[54] The next session of the General Assembly remedied that situation. Chapter 202 of the Acts of 1959 affected all Indiana school corporations, regardless of whether they had already reorganized. It established a Commission for the Reorganization of School Corporations to adopt minimum standards for proposed school reorganizations and to aid county committees in examining plans.[55]

The 1960s promised many changes in Indiana's education system. Two major reforms—school consolidations and curriculum revisions—were linked to the future and fortunes of the Indiana Junior Historical Society.

CHAPTER 3

Members and Activities Multiply

The Indiana Junior Historical Society had a full-time, state-funded executive director by 1965. In keeping with the organization's history, the process by which this occurred involved incremental steps and the cooperation of several groups.

Carl Zenor continued to work part time to attract new member clubs to the IJHS, while he also led Indiana's Civil War Centennial Commission. He left the Indiana Historical Bureau at the end of 1963 to head the Indiana Sesquicentennial Commission beginning in January 1964. Prior to his departure Zenor indicated that responsibility for the IJHS had passed to Robert J. Montgomery as of September 1962.[1]

Montgomery's ties to the juniors dated back to at least 1958, when the history club he sponsored at Sandcreek High School in Decatur County was selected as the outstanding IJHS member club.[2] In January 1962 Hubert H. Hawkins named Montgomery, by then a history instructor at Harrison Township High School in Delaware County, as the first director of the IJHS, albeit on a part-time basis.[3] Zenor was still on the Bureau staff at that time, so Mont-

gomery's salary was paid by the Indiana Historical Society and the Society of Indiana Pioneers.[4]

Funding from the two private agencies, while generous, was not permanent. Montgomery continued to teach full time through the 1962–63 school year. Although he was put on the state payroll as an hourly employee at the Bureau in February 1964, supplements were still necessary from the two societies. Neither organization, however, was prepared to underwrite the program indefinitely.[5] Hawkins reported in 1965 that state senator Robert O'Bannon had "secured the addition of $10,000 to the Bureau's budget," which allowed Hawkins to make Montgomery a full-time state employee.[6] In the minutes of the Indiana Library and Historical Board dated 27 July 1965 Hawkins again credited O'Bannon for the appropriations needed for Montgomery "to promote the Junior Historical Society movement in Indiana and to act as a liaison man."

Montgomery's arrival marked the beginning of a period of expansion and innovation for the IJHS. A revised constitution adopted in 1962 permitted the creation of junior high clubs, something the leadership had advocated since 1949.[7] When the junior high clubs affiliated, they came in as the junior division of the IJHS. The high school members comprised the senior division. In 1966 additional changes allowed chapters from the fourth, fifth, and sixth grades to be chartered.

A new source of adult support for the IJHS was an advisory board created by Hawkins in 1965 and made up of a dozen or more individuals from across the state who counseled Montgomery and his young colleagues, particularly on financial matters.

The potential growth of the IJHS was dependent on the number of schools available to join. As mentioned in Chapter 2, between the late 1950s and mid-1960s, Indiana's education reformers were busy attempting to consolidate school districts, revise curriculum requirements, and marshal the legislative and bureaucratic support necessary for both.

There were 3,347 schools open in Indiana between 1936 and 1942. By the 1960–61 school year the total number of schools in Indiana had dropped to 2,325.[8] Part of this decrease can be attributed to the school consolidation movement that began in 1959. The policy of the Commission for the Reorganization of School Corporations between 1959 and 1965 was to complete reorganizations as soon as possible. By 1 January 1965, 80 percent of all public school students in the state were enrolled in reorganized school districts of adequate size.[9]

The 1965 General Assembly extended the Reorganization Act to 1969. In 1967 the commission reported that 156 of the state's school corporations were too small to provide minimum school programs. By 1 January 1968 Indiana had 382 public school corporations, down from 940 in 1959.[10]

The consolidation of many rural school districts brought stability to the pool of potential IJHS member clubs. Records indicate that the IJHS could claim 49 member clubs as of December 1963, and 173 clubs by September 1967.[11] By 1972 the junior society claimed nearly 12,000 members in an estimated 210 active clubs for young people in grades four through twelve.[12] The IJHS, the first organization of its kind in the United States, was also the largest by 1971.[13]

Since 1920 most schoolchildren in Indiana had been exposed to the state's history in seventh or eighth grade. By the 1950s, however, some educators wanted to change the social studies curriculum to progress "from matters of purely local interest to state or regional history, then to American history," according to records of the Department of Public Instruction.[14] In 1960 guidelines stated that intermediate grades should be familiar with places of historical interest in Indiana and that students should know "a great deal about the history, geography, peoples, and industry of Indiana, our nation, and the other parts of the world."[15] Clearly, many influential professional educators in Indiana sought to teach state history earlier than in junior high. In the curriculum reform movement, the Indiana Junior Historical Society promoted changes to enhance the teaching of Indiana history and opposed efforts to decrease its importance.

In the fall of 1960 Superintendent of Public Instruction William E. Wilson appointed a special committee to make

Robert Montgomery with Beverly Nasser of the Wabash Valley Supplementary Education Center. *Richard H. Bruce*

(Top) Senator Robert O'Bannon. *Who's Who and What's What in Indiana Politics* (Indianapolis: James E. Perry, 1944)

(Bottom) Robert Montgomery at 1962 IJHS Workshop (left to right: Glenn Neeves, Montgomery, Arville Funk). *Indiana Historical Bureau*

recommendations for revisions in the social studies curriculum for Indiana's public schools.[16] The report of the State Social Studies Curriculum Revision Committee to Wilson, dated 13 September 1963, included the following provisions:

- recommended Indiana history be taught in fourth grade
- removed Indiana history from the middle school curriculum
- included Indiana history as an elective at the high school level

IJHS officers, on behalf of their federation of seventy-five clubs representing more than three thousand students, responded on 27 April 1964, asking Superintendent Wilson to "submit to the Indiana General Education Commission our request that they reject the plan to be submitted for the revision of the Social Studies Curriculum in Indiana Schools." Officers stated that the removal of the junior high Indiana history course "would do irreparable harm to the future welfare of the state of Indiana."[17] Minutes of the Indiana Library and Historical Board and State Board of Education meetings also mentioned the controversy. Hubert Hawkins said that removing Indiana history from the eighth grade curriculum was ill-advised because "Indiana history is a part of American history."[18]

On 2 May 1964 delegates to the annual convention of the IJHS drafted a resolution signed by the officers to send to the governor at the beginning of the 1965 General As-sembly stating that "the Legislature should make it mandatory that completion of a one semester course in Indiana History be required for graduation from a commissioned high school of the State of Indiana." Records indicate that "a bill was then introduced in the 1965 General Assembly to make such a course mandatory, but it received little consideration."[19]

In a November 1965 memo to all superintendents and principals, Edgar B. Smith, assistant state superintendent for instructional services, confirmed that the recommendations for grades K–7 submitted by the Commission of General Education had been approved by the Indiana State Board of Education in June 1965.[20] United States history would be taught in grades 8 and 11. In July 1965 the board had approved a proposal to offer Indiana history as an elective course in grades 9 through 12.[21]

The tenacious officers of the IJHS pushed legislators one more time, in 1967, to enact House Bill 1094, which "provides . . . that public high schools holding a First Class Commission must offer a one semester elective course in Indiana history." In endorsing the bill, Thomas S. Emison, president of the Indiana Historical Society, said he hoped it would receive "sympathetic consideration and . . . a favorable committee report."[22] The bill passed in the House but failed in the Senate. "I am going to be at a loss to offer any explanation to the seven thousand members of our organization as to why this bill was not considered by the Senate Education Committee, since you, Chairman of the Committee and also a member of our Advisory Council, did agree with Representative [Robert W.] Gordon to be a

Senate sponsor of the bill if it passed the House, and since the bill was introduced in the Senate under your co-sponsorship," IJHS Secretary Debbie Cramer wrote to Sen. J. J. Bailey after the setback.[23]

In his response to Cramer, Bailey rejected Representative Gordon's claim. "I told him that in principle I did not favor it. I did not promise him that I would be the sponsor of it. As I see it, a high school curriculum should be determined by the State Department of Education," said Bailey. Stating that several education groups and university professors had opposed the bill, Bailey listed loss of accreditation for high schools that did not teach Indiana history, lack of teacher preparation and adequate textbooks, "woefully inadequate" resources on Indiana history in many high school libraries, and opportunities to learn Indiana history in American history or civics classes as justifications for his decision.

"I am aware that the study of Indiana history has great value in causing one to have an appreciation of our Hoosier heritage. I am confident that your organization is playing a very important role in this regard. Keep up the good work!" Bailey said to Cramer.[24] Likewise, the *Indiana History Bulletin* stated, "Regardless of the outcome IJHS members are to be commended upon a demonstration of responsible interest and initiative."[25]

Although this involvement in real politics must have been instructive in itself for the junior leaders, they faced two major challenges with the implementation of curriculum changes: to support elementary schoolteachers and students in their study of Indiana history, and to develop new ways to make Indiana history interesting to teenagers who were no longer required to study it in junior high and high school.

Prior to the legislature's actions, Hawkins had recognized the Bureau's responsibility to organize a separate program directed at elementary children. Accordingly, "in September 1966 the Indiana Junior Historical Society began issuing charters to elementary schools for chapters of 'The Little Hoosier Historian' organization," which was restricted to grades four, five, or six, or any combination of the three.[26] The first Little Hoosier chapter was chartered on 12 September 1966 at Westwood School in Batesville.[27] By June 1967 the IJHS could claim twenty chapters serving approximately eight hundred students.[28]

Unlike the high school and junior high school clubs, which were extracurricular, the Little Hoosier chapters often consisted of fourth-grade classes meeting during the school day. This helped to account for the steady growth of the division. The organization for the Little Hoosier Historian division generally followed that of the older divisions. The chapters, while usually school-sponsored, could be supervised by libraries, museums, or local historical societies, so long as there were adult leaders. Each group paid a charter fee of one dollar per year, while annual dues were twenty-five cents per child.[29]

At the state level, instead of electing a president and other officers, the Little Hoosiers elected a Statewide Council made up of eight members, four representing the fifth grade and four representing the sixth grade. One representative from each grade level was elected from each quar-

Flora History Club officers and sponsors display the sesquicentennial bumper plate. *Glen Dillman*

(Top) Junior historians updated information about markers such as this one for the 1966 edition of the *Directory of Historical Markers in Indiana*, published by the Indiana Historical Bureau. *Indiana Historical Bureau*

(Bottom) Juniors traveled to Vincennes in 1964. *Indiana Historical Bureau*

ter of the state. At the time of the spring state convention, candidates who were entering the fifth and sixth grades in the next school year competed for statewide council positions. Plans for the next spring convention originated with the statewide council as did other Little Hoosier state activities during the year.[30]

Among IJHS membership benefits were newsletters published four times during the school year; opportunities to participate in writing contests, exhibit days, and tours of historic interest; and access to speakers and Montgomery's consulting and planning services.

Beginning in 1969 the IJHS offered a weekend workshop every February for elementary schoolteachers. Some 100 to 150 teachers attended the workshops, conducted by IJHS staff persons and Little Hoosier sponsors. Teachers building a new course of study were eager to learn all they could about Indiana history, folklore, and geography. The workshops not only guided them to specific resources but also described how to make history interesting to elementary students. These workshops became a means of recruiting for the Little Hoosier Historian organization. Many of the elementary teachers became excellent Little Hoosier sponsors, deeply committed to the success of the junior historical movement in Indiana.

Although the IJHS was flourishing with many new Little Hoosier chapters and junior and senior high school clubs, it still lacked independent stature and a budget. The director's salary and administrative costs were covered by the Bureau, and funds for other projects came from a variety of private sources. However, state funding for the director's

position alone was not adequate for what Hawkins and Montgomery expected to accomplish. The General Assembly would not support a struggling association of a few scattered clubs. Since older students were not required to study Indiana history, Montgomery needed to create a variety of appealing activities to sustain individual clubs and the IJHS as a whole. To get the financial backing the movement badly needed, the IJHS had to grow significantly and demonstrate that it was providing valuable services to the state.

Preparations for the 1966 celebration of Indiana's sesquicentennial of statehood provided several opportunities for the IJHS. Longtime supporter Carl Zenor was still executive director of the statewide Sesquicentennial Commission. When the General Assembly created the nineteen-member commission in 1957, organizers had agreed that programs should be aimed especially at school-age Hoosiers.[31] Both junior and senior division members served on the IJHS Sesquicentennial Committee. Opportunities for student involvement included selling commemorative items, compiling information about historical markers, and collecting valuable manuscripts.

With the approval of the state officers, the IJHS offered member clubs the opportunity to purchase sesquicentennial booster plates on consignment from the Indiana Historical Society. The blue and gold front bumper plates, which displayed the torch and stars from the state's flag, sold for ninety-eight cents, plus two cents tax. Clubs were allowed to keep twenty-five cents from the sale of each plate.[32]

By October 1964 the IJHS chapter at Arlington High School in Indianapolis had sold three hundred plates and was working on its second order.[33] The *IJHS Newsletter* reported on 30 November 1964 that many clubs found that selling bumper plates was an easy way to make money. The junior club sponsored by the Allen County–Fort Wayne Historical Society conducted a one-day sale of the plates at a shopping center in April 1965, with radio station WOWO providing on-air promotion.[34]

The Bureau enlisted the help of the junior society in one of its mandated responsibilities—management of the historical markers near Indiana highways. For decades the Bureau had administered the purchase and placement of the cast aluminum markers. The most recent compilation of markers had been published in January 1929 as the third edition of *Historical Markers and Public Memorials in Indiana*.[35] The juniors project, which began in January 1964, involved contacting key persons in all ninety-two counties for updated marker information and then compiling the data.[36] Students who worked on the markers project included IJHS Sesquicentennial Committee members Anna Jane Miller, Harrison Township High School; Mike Westfall, Allen County–Fort Wayne Junior Historical Society; Kenneth Neeley, Fountain Central High School; Benny Clarke, Ben Davis High School; Margo Edson, Kokomo High School; Bill Fish, Columbus Northside Junior High School; Prudence Stallings, New Harmony Guild of Guides; and Vicki Gray, Peru High School.[37]

The work of these students resulted in the 1966 Bureau publication, *Directory of Historical Markers in Indiana,* and a supplement the next year. Both documents were special issues of the *Indiana History Bulletin.* Montgomery believed that the directory would be one of the most important contributions any group could make to the sesquicentennial observance.[38]

With the markers publication completed, members of the IJHS Sesquicentennial Committee were ready to participate in a much larger undertaking—the statewide "Hunting Hoosier History" project, administered by the Indiana State Library. Directed by Thomas K. Krasean, then field representative for the library, the project sought to preserve historically significant documents. The Indiana Sesquicentennial Commission asked all Hoosiers to submit, for either reproduction or permanent donation, letters, diaries, oral reminiscences, sermons, speeches, and business records. Officials expected the endeavor to locate and preserve at least eighty thousand manuscripts, and all acceptable documents would be included in a log to be distributed to libraries in the state.[39] "At this significant point in Hoosier history, it is especially appropriate that Hoosiers make a strenuous effort to preserve as much of our documentary heritage as possible," stated a promotional flyer.

Gov. Roger D. Branigin announced that awards would be given to the three counties that made the most significant contributions to the manuscript project, scheduled to run from 1 March 1966 to 30 April 1967. A first prize of one thousand dollars, second prize of five hundred dollars, and third prize of two hundred dollars would go to the groups responsible for the collections, based on the number of pages contributed in relation to the age and population of their counties.[40]

Ohio River architectural survey with the Kentucky Junior Historical Society.
Indiana Historical Bureau

(Top) Dyan Bricker of Marion was elected president of the Indiana Junior Historical Society in 1967. *Indiana Historical Bureau*

(Bottom) At the 1966 Midwest Conference of Junior Historians in Vincennes were, from left to right, Mrs. Ramsey, Glenn Bertels, Anna Jane Miller, Mayor Earl Lawson, Ann Turner, and Bob Montgomery. *Indiana Historical Bureau*

IJHS Sesquicentennial Committee members were assigned specific groups of high school clubs through which to solicit documents. The junior society announced that cash prizes of fifty, twenty-five, and fifteen dollars would be awarded to clubs that produced the highest number of acceptable pages.[41] IJHS members who worked on the manuscript project included Russ Bultman, Arlington; Kenneth Neeley, Fountain Central; Deborah Doan, Noblesville Junior High School; Jim Greene, Muncie Central; Sharon Tolley, Twin Lakes; Margo Edson, Kokomo; Martha Jarvis, Union; Mike Carnighan, Scribner; Molly Head, Columbus Northside; Carol Lynn Doup, Columbus; Johnie Williamson, Hamilton Heights; and Mike Westfall, Allen County–Fort Wayne.[42]

By July 1967 Krasean reported that more than forty-two thousand pages of materials had been copied. At an awards dinner on 28 June 1967 winners from Washington (first), Franklin (second), and Hendricks (third) Counties received their prizes.[43]

The Indiana Historical Society announced plans in 1967 to continue the manuscript collection process under the direction of William E. Wilson, former superintendent of public instruction.[44] The *IJHS Newsletter* reported in May 1968 that Rossville and Rushville Junior High Schools were winners of the manuscript competition for the juniors.

Spring and fall pilgrimages, instituted in 1964, forged closer ties among clubs and members. Tours were usually scheduled in October and April. Member clubs paid their expenses and furnished transportation. Sometimes buses were provided, depending on the tour and the number of participants.

One of the most popular pilgrimages was in 1964 to Vincennes, the oldest city in Indiana and former capital of the Indiana Territory. The pilgrimage introduced students to landmarks of early Indiana: Grouseland, home of William Henry Harrison; the old territorial capitol; the Old Cathedral, now the Basilica of St. Francis Xavier; Elihu Stout's *Western Sun* print shop; and the George Rogers Clark Memorial. Other tours took the juniors to Fort Ouiatenon in Lafayette, and to Corydon, New Harmony, the Limberlost region in northern Indiana, and Fort Recovery in Ohio. Destinations depended on what clubs were interested and how far they wished to travel.

History clubs often acted as hosts for pilgrimages to their areas. In the spring of 1966 a group of 150 juniors in four buses, emblazoned with IJHS banners contributed by the WOWO radio station, visited Fort Wayne.[45] In a combined walking and bus tour conducted by Mike Westfall and other members of the Allen County Historical Museum's history club, students explored the museum, Johnny Appleseed's grave, the old commercial district, and the actual fort named for General Anthony Wayne, Revolutionary War hero and leader of the victorious forces at the 1794 Battle of Fallen Timbers.

In 1967 the Knights of History, the history club at Arlington High School in Indianapolis, conducted a tour of the capital city for more than three hundred visitors from fifteen schools. The route was based on the well-known Riley Trail, a self-guided tour in which thirty-three historical points were marked by a profile of James Whitcomb Riley. Under the leadership of sponsor John Holmes, Arlington club members produced an illuminated map of the trail and a guidebook as a community service. Each guide on the tour "was prepared to add background information to bring the on-the-spot learning experience to life and make the historic pilgrimage as meaningful as possible."[46]

One of the most significant IJHS summer programs for the junior-senior division involved a series of architectural surveys projected to extend over a ten-year period beginning in 1967. Seventeen members of the first architectural survey committee met at Clifty Falls State Park from 28 to 30 September 1967 to plan the survey series, study the architecture around Madison, and prepare a guidebook.[47] The result was *A Brief Guide for an Architectural Survey of Indiana,* published in 1968. It was adapted from Wilbur D. Peat's 1962 book on Indiana architecture.[48]

Mike Westfall became leader of the initial survey effort after striking a deal with Montgomery. In the spring of 1967 Westfall had been a candidate for the IJHS presidency against Dyan Bricker from Marion, but a term paper on nineteenth-century architecture in Fort Wayne had sparked his interest in Montgomery's latest brainstorm. The IJHS director told Westfall that he could head up the new project if he would withdraw from the election and throw his support to Bricker.[49]

Houses, churches, schools, and business buildings dating to the nineteenth century could be found in many Indiana towns. Montgomery's original idea was to take a survey team of junior historians into a selected community for a week to photograph and document its architecture. The students would learn to identify architectural styles and de-termine the historical significance of the buildings. Students would interview residents and record such factual data as construction dates and the names of the original and present owners. The IJHS would publish survey findings in a booklet. The architectural projects paralleled activities in New York, New Jersey, Wisconsin, and Kentucky, according to the October 1969 issue of the *National Junior Historian Newsletter.*

The number of juniors participating in each survey was limited to about twelve students. After Montgomery selected the location for a summer's project, he issued a call for interested applicants through the IJHS newsletter. Though club members at a survey site might be included, generally the teams were made up of young people from elsewhere in the state. Montgomery tried for a balance of boys and girls, representatives of big schools and smaller ones, and members from both northern and southern Indiana. "He went to great lengths to match the right people, and he sometimes sought out kids who needed the project more than the project needed them," said Westfall. "Bob saw the IJHS as a place to teach people to be leaders and to interact with others."[50]

Joining each survey team were adults who had ties to the IJHS, usually sponsors who worked during the summer for the IJHS. IJHS alumni were often included, particularly after the establishment of an alumni association in 1969. The older students and the adults aided the high school historians with their photographs and survey forms and tried to keep all facets of the survey on schedule.[51]

Fort Ouiatenon dig, 1969. *Indiana Historical Bureau*

(Top) Site of Lockport dig. *Indiana Historical Bureau*

(Bottom) The "chain gang" prepares to begin work at the Lockport dig site. *Indiana Historical Bureau*

The first town survey was conducted in Vernon, the seat of Jennings County in southeastern Indiana. Eleven students and four adults, including Montgomery, took part in that initial undertaking in the summer of 1968. It began "with the meticulous task of numerically mapping every building in the community." The map, created by Polly Hendricks, Jon Hubbard, and Julie Johnson of the Vernon Junior High School History Club, was reprinted in the 1968 pamphlet of building photographs.[52]

After a bad emulsion spoiled all the original photographs for the Vernon publication, Westfall, by then a high school graduate, was forced to retake shots of the 105 residences, 17 store buildings, 7 offices, 1 public building, 1 factory, and various human interest elements.[53] In the text, students noted that geographic boundaries of the small town were unchanged since 1851, but that Vernon's 1968 population of 431 represented a drop in the number of inhabitants. Local contractor Homer Dell told the students: "If you want to get rich, get out of Jennings County. If you want to live, stay in Vernon."[54]

The first of four Rush County studies, also made during the summer of 1968, took place in conjunction with the first annual Festival of the Arts held in Homer. Along with workshops on music, art, and creative writing, festival planners wanted to include a workshop on history.

Al Hodge, the Rushville High School history club sponsor, invited the IJHS to conduct the four-day history workshop. In the opening session Montgomery furnished background on basic types of nineteenth-century architecture. Local students gave a slide program, highlighting points of interest in Rush County. Then the IJHS students divided into small survey teams to traverse the roads of Walker Township, photographing old buildings and recording historical data. On the last night of the workshop they joined the people of Homer for folksinging and a pitch-in supper.

Although the IJHS did not conduct another history workshop at the Homer Festival, survey teams from Rushville High School continued the Rush County project during the next three summers of the festival, completing all townships in the county by 1971.

Montgomery engaged in considerable planning for the surveys. He drove all the county roads, pinpointing the buildings worth recording. True to his schoolteacher background, he planned the routes and assignments so that the students would discover for themselves what he wanted them to find. With asterisks and notations on their maps, he directed them to good architectural examples. If they missed one, he might send them back with clearer instructions.[55]

For most of the IJHS architectural surveys, the students' work continued beyond the actual on-site project. Several team members served as editors, writing copy and designing layouts for the booklets. Some editing sessions took place at state parks. For other booklets, the student editors met at Conklin House, Montgomery's home in Cambridge City.

The results of the 1969 Oldenburg survey were published in a twenty-four-page booklet titled *Oldenburg: The Village of Spires,* and printed in 1970. The study examined the early life and customs of this German community where the architecture reflected a European tradition. This study was unique in that it was made in December during a Christmas break rather than in the summer.[56]

The 1969–70 annual report of the Indiana Historical Bureau noted that the IJHS architectural surveys had elicited favorable comments from the National Park Service and the American Institute of Architects.[57]

The 1972 Wabash River trip was a historic tour as well as a study of architecture. In late June the IJHS survey group traced the Wabash River from its source in Jay County to Posey County where it empties into the Ohio River. Thomas K. Krasean, then archivist at Vincennes University, was one of the adults accompanying Montgomery and the IJHS members on this project.

A study in 1972 examined water crossings in southeastern Indiana, a project sponsored with the Society of Indiana Pioneers. In other studies, students focused on a particular kind of building, such as the churches of Cass County or the schoolhouses of Posey County. In the Cass County project, which the Society of Indiana Pioneers also funded, student team members interviewed ministers, trustees, and older members of church congregations. They studied the architecture of more than eighty country, small town, and city churches in the county.

"Almost all of the churches of the traditional denominations were found to be of the Gothic style of architecture, either of the type made famous by Sir Christopher Wren when he designed the Old North Church of Boston, a rectangular building with a central vestry and steeple and spire, or of the style we have termed Tudor Gothic, having a square tower, usually flat topped and with battlements," explained the students in the introduction to *A View of Ecclesiastical Architecture in Cass County, Indiana,* published in 1972.

Three high school groups carried out the 1971 Posey County schoolhouse study: the history clubs of Mount Vernon and North Posey high schools and the Guild of Guides of New Harmony.

One of the last architectural projects under Montgomery's direction was a study of Indiana barns and other farm buildings in 1973 and 1974, also in cooperation with the Society of Indiana Pioneers. Montgomery wanted the three groups of young people for this survey to understand changes in rural Indiana up to 1920, when mechanized farming transformed the use of barns. "After that time barns no longer needed to provide space for work animals, and the need for haylofts was eliminated except in dairy barns," students explained in their booklet. In separate projects, students examined four representative areas of the state: De Kalb County in the northeast, Benton County in the northwest, Henry County in central Indiana, and Scott and Jefferson Counties in the southeast.

Students discovered that the farm buildings usually reflected the agriculture of the regions. A De Kalb County dairy farmer had to "provide storage for a vast amount of hay, as well as a milkshed," while a southeastern Hoosier farmer needed not only shelter for work animals and their feed, but also "space for curing tobacco." After the IJHS published the survey booklet in 1975, titled *Barns and Other Outbuildings on Indiana Farms,* the collection of nearly five hundred photographs with survey data was given to the Indiana Historical Society's library.[58]

Architectural interest stimulated by IJHS survey projects prompted several local clubs to study the early architecture in their own communities and prepare booklets that the IJHS published and included in its collection. The first of these were the New Harmony, Liberty, and Vevay surveys, all completed in 1969. Later publications were done by history clubs at Centerville, Knightstown, and Connersville. Local businesses and townspeople supported these ventures, with Montgomery's help. In the Liberty study, renowned Indianapolis architect H. Roll McLaughlin served as editorial adviser.[59]

Indiana juniors joined teams from other states to conduct additional surveys. They teamed with the Kentucky Young Historians to study architecture and history on both sides of the Ohio River in 1969, focusing mainly on smaller communities that tended "to retain more evidences of the past era of River culture."[60] Originally intended as a one-week cruise downriver from Madison to Mount Vernon, the tour changed to a motorcade when boat accommodations could not be arranged.

Twelve teenagers made the trip, eight from the IJHS and four from Kentucky, accompanied by four adults.[61] Participants were impressed not only by the architecture and decor of homes but also by river folklore and conversations with older residents. A high point of interest was McHarry's tomb where, supposedly, a ferryboat operator was buried upright in a glass coffin so that he could swear at steamboat pilots when they passed by.[62]

The next year a team from Indiana and Kentucky traveled the Lincoln Heritage Trail for another combined architectural study and historical tour, beginning at Springfield, Kentucky, the home of Abraham Lincoln's father, Thomas. On their ten-day trip they followed the route past Lincoln landmarks in Indiana and then crossed the Wabash River at Vincennes. At Charleston, Illinois, four Illinois high school students and their sponsor joined them. The trail ended at New Salem and Springfield, Illinois, where the mature Abraham Lincoln had lived. All along the route the young surveyors were photographing, researching, and interviewing for their study of homes built in the lifetimes of the two Lincolns, before and during the Civil War.[63]

Another tristate effort, in 1971, focused on three towns of Shelbyville, each located in Shelby Counties of Indiana, Illinois, and Kentucky. All named for the first Kentucky governor, Isaac Shelby, the three areas were agricultural communities of similar size. The purpose of this study, in addition to documenting historical buildings, was to determine if any influence from Kentucky could be found in the counterpart communities in Indiana and Illinois. In part, persons migrating from Kentucky had settled the latter two areas.

"Nowhere were buildings found that could be said to have been patterned after those seen in the preceding state," wrote the students in their subsequent publication. "However the study did reveal a progression of the influences of styles of architecture as we traveled westward." Students also commented that buildings classified as "pure" examples of architectural styles were rare west of the Alleghenies.[64]

In 1972 another tristate survey concentrated on southwestern Indiana and neighboring areas of Kentucky and Illinois, familiar territory to Montgomery, who had grown up in Posey County. Young historians from three states, five each from Indiana and Illinois and four from Kentucky, traveled to two counties in each state. "A poignant feeling of seeing the real places touched each one of us. . . . Meeting people during interviews and driving down dusty backroads to unusual places presented quite a new experience for each of us sometime during the trip," recounted Susie Orrahood of the Kentucky Young Historians. As in the other surveys, the results were published in a booklet, written and compiled by a student editorial committee.[65]

In addition to the joint architectural projects, the IJHS organized annual conferences and gatherings of students from other states. In March 1963 the first Midwest Conference of Junior Historians took place in Indianapolis under the direction of the IJHS. Montgomery initiated this conference to encourage the local junior history clubs to exchange ideas and broaden their focus.[66] Representatives came from Ohio, Illinois, Kentucky, and Wisconsin. Reflecting the activism of the Indiana students in curriculum reform at that time, delegates passed a resolution urging the state legislators in Indiana, Illinois, and Kentucky to require courses in state history for high school graduation. The 1966 conference took place in Vincennes.

The IJHS founded the *National Junior Historian Newsletter* in December 1966 and published it until April 1972.[67] It featured articles about the other state junior historical groups as well as information about the Indiana program.[68]

Additional evidence of Montgomery's creative approach to teaching history was in his organization of summer archaeological digs. The Indiana Historical Society's 1967 publication of Glenn A. Black's two-volume *Angel Site: An Archaeological, Historical, and Ethnological Site*, a summary of the excavation of 191 acres and eleven mounds in the 400-acre site in Vanderburgh County in the late 1930s and early 1940s, presumably influenced the IJHS's choice of archaeology as a new activity.[69] The Society's interest in archaeology dated to the 1930s when Eli Lilly's enthusiasm and financial resources made possible a comprehensive effort to unearth and document Indiana's rich archaeological heritage. The Indiana Historical Bureau published a number of reports of the Society's archaeological findings.

The first IJHS dig, in July 1969, took place near Lafayette, at the site of Fort Ouiatenon, a French trading post established in 1717. Seven juniors joined a team of college students under the direction of James H. Kellar, an Indiana University professor of anthropology and Glenn Black's successor as the Society's archaeologist. Kellar assigned the high schoolers to dig in a cornfield in the floodplain of the Wabash River on a humid summer day.

Marlesa (Marcy) Gray was not yet a junior in high school when she participated in the dig at Fort Ouiatenon, but she decided within the week on archaeology as a career. She became a student of Kellar's at Indiana University, earning an undergraduate degree there and a master's degree from Michigan State University. She directed several other early junior digs. Later she wrote the archaeological monograph *The Archaeological Investigations of Fort Knox II,*

In 1978 the Indiana Junior Historical Society published *Readin, Writin, and Rithmetic: The Story of Goddard School*. Included in the booklet were excerpts from the students' interviews with former Goddard School pupils, conducted as part of an oral history project coordinated by IJHS sponsor Al Hodge. In explaining the purposes of oral history, Hodge said, "People a century from now are much less likely to be able to go to their grandmother's attic and find stacks of letters dated circa 1978. One way to help fill this gap is by tape recording interviews with people who haven't saved their correspondence for a lifetime nor maintained a multi-volume diary but who have a wealth of memories about their experiences and their times." *Indiana Historical Bureau*

After the award ceremony honoring her winning description of the Goddard School project, Marcy McDowell was photographed on the steps of the Capitol in Washington, D. C., with, from left to right, Robert Kirby, and then Indiana congressmen William Bray and William H. Hudnut III. *Indiana Historical Bureau*

Knox County, Indiana, 1803–1813, described below, for the Indiana Historical Society. Gray later opened her own archaeological firm in Cincinnati, Ohio.[70]

The 1970 archaeological activity involved outlining the foundations of old Fort Knox II near Vincennes during two one-week camps. American soldiers had occupied the fort from about 1803 to 1813 "when the War of 1812 prompted its return to the town of Vincennes as a protection to the inhabitants."[71] Glenn A. Black had located the site in the early 1960s. The IJHS team for the first week dug small trenches, following the markings that located the stockade walls. Using crushed limestone, the second group delineated the boundaries of the old fort. The project was intended "to allow visitors to form a more accurate mental picture of the original fort and to lay groundwork for more extensive restoration in the future by the Indiana Historical Society[—]owners of the site."[72] The high school students also took side trips to historical sites in Vincennes.[73]

Another excavation project was made possible through the IJHS Alumni Association, which was organized in 1969 "to further the study of the history of Indiana and to assist in the preservation of Hoosier and American heritages by advancing the IJHS in all possible and honorable ways."[74] As an incorporated body, the alumni association could hold any property the junior society might acquire. A later purpose was to increase memberships.

On behalf of the IJHS, in 1971 the alumni association acquired ten acres in Vigo County just north of the town of Riley for three thousand dollars from Mrs. Guy Archer of Phoenix, Arizona, who purchased the property with her late husband at a tax sale in 1949.[75] On this property, known as Lockport, were traces of the Wabash and Erie Canal, the 460-mile water route that had been built from 1832 to 1853 to link Lake Erie at Toledo, Ohio, with the Ohio River at Evansville.[76]

The idea for acquiring the land originated in the early 1960s with the history club at Terre Haute's Wiley High School.[77] For almost ten years the club worked to realize its goal, first with financial support from the Lions Club at Riley. From numerous fund-raising efforts and donations the IJHS raised twenty-four hundred dollars of the three thousand dollar purchase price. The remaining six hundred dollars was secured through a loan from the Hoosier State Bank at Hammond.[78]

By 1971 nothing of the canal was left but the towpath crossing the entire property, parts of the canal bed, and one lock wall still in good condition. A highway cut off the stretch of the canal bed in one direction and a drainage ditch blocked it in the other. The juniors intended to restore the lock, refill the channel, and create an impression of the canal as it once was.[79]

The project required several years' work. The first crew of IJHS volunteers started work in November 1971, clearing the fallen timber, weeds, and underbrush that obscured the towpath.[80] In subsequent summers other groups spent a week at work camps at the site. Once a trail was opened the students began to dig out the lock. Students followed painstaking archaeological processes but uncovered relatively few artifacts. They did, however, find the bottom of the lock, made of white oak.

Work on Lockport went on until 1975. In July 1974 Montgomery sought additional funds from the Indiana Chemical Trust and the Frederick R. Benson Trust at Terre Haute: "We have now come to the place where it seems desirable to erect a primitive like building, simulating a keeper's lock house. This would be preferably a log cabin. . . . It will have a fireplace, no other furnishings, and could then be used by club sponsors who wished to show the students something of pioneer living, by spending a night or a weekend living as pioneers did. . . . The cabin could also be used to house high school students doing volunteer work on the property."[81]

Montgomery estimated the cost at one thousand dollars and asked for financial assistance "since the IJHS has no financing except gifts." The money was not forthcoming, the proposed cabin was never built, and nothing more substantial was done in restoring the lock.[82] The IJHS Alumni Association still owns the property, but no further work has been carried out.

The restoration of the Goddard School at Homer was another IJHS achievement during Montgomery's tenure. The Goddard School was built in 1885 for the students of Walker Township School District No. One.[83] Goddard (whose first name was apparently not recorded) owned the land on which the school was built and charged the school one dollar per year for use of the property. The land was to be returned to Goddard's heirs when it was no longer maintained for the school.

The property was eventually sold to Rue Miller. In 1973 the Gene Miller family entered into a ten-year lease, renewable for two ten-year periods, with the IJHS that permitted the junior group to restore and operate the property. Funding for the restoration project was provided by Lotus Miller, a successful businessman from Cambridge City and former Goddard student; James Associates; and Lilly Endowment.

Except for the major construction work, all the restoration was done by IJHS members during 1973 and 1974. Participants included students from clubs at Rushville, Connersville, Knightstown, Brownsburg, and Thomas Carr Howe High School in Indianapolis. When the restored 1885 Goddard schoolhouse was dedicated on 8 June 1975 the original school bell was hanging in the reconstructed belfry. A potbellied stove, old desks of different sizes, inkwells, and textbooks from the period accentuated the restoration.

Marcy McDowell, a student from Howe High School, submitted the Goddard School project in a contest cosponsored by the *American Girl* magazine and the National Trust for Historic Preservation. She was notified on 24 April 1974 that the submission won first place, bringing the IJHS national accolades and a check for one hundred dollars from *American Girl*.[84] At the award ceremony on 7 May 1974 in Washington, D.C., the students were recognized for showing "initiative and imagination in restoring with documented authenticity a one-room schoolhouse, and thus . . . preserving for their contemporaries a piece of Americana familiar to their grandparents."[85] After the ceremony McDowell was photographed on the steps of the United States Capitol with Robert Kirby, assistant IJHS director, and Indiana congressmen William Bray and William H. Hudnut III.

The school was maintained by Rush County groups for a time as a museum. Knightstown and Carthage students helped clean up the building and grounds each spring, and for several years Rushville High School history club members kept it open on Sunday afternoons. As part of their study of Indiana history, many elementary schoolchildren in the area have taken part in a half-day of old-time education at Goddard School.

CHAPTER 4

New Clubs and State Events Unfold

The Indiana Junior Historical Society program was strengthened by year-round contact with the school clubs. The summer programs maintained the interest of clubs and individual members when schools were not in session. However, the tours, surveys, camps, and digs involved only a fraction of the total IJHS membership. Summer participants were encouraged to stimulate their clubs during the school year.

The real strength of the IJHS was in the two hundred school clubs and their members. Bob Montgomery knew that any ideas originating in the Indiana Historical Bureau would fall flat if they had no appeal to club members throughout the state. If clubs were not kept interested and active they would disappear, and the IJHS would wither.

The 1966 handbook for officers and club sponsors made the intent clear: "The club is for the benefit and enjoyment of its members. . . . The officers should be responsible for insisting that the club program be carried out by the members, and should insist that all members participate in the various activities. Every member should have

something to do during the year, other than just attending meetings."[1]

In the fall of 1962 the IJHS began publishing the *IJHS Newsletter,* containing information about scheduled events, newly chartered clubs, individual club projects, trips, and other activities. Montgomery had difficulty getting responses from the clubs and generating students' participation in the newsletter. Since the 1940s the IJHS had experienced uneven success with its publications.

In January 1963 the Indiana Historical Bureau began publishing the *Hoosier Historian,* an annual booklet of student writings on state and local history. Free to clubs, it was at first published annually, then later biannually. Editors announced plans in April 1970 for a new magazine of the same title to be issued three times during the school year at a club subscription rate of one dollar. Writing was no longer limited to students.

The change to a new magazine was prompted by the poor rating given the *National Junior Historian Newsletter.* Of the seven or eight publications examined, the IJHS magazine ranked lowest. Unfortunately, the new *Hoosier Historian* was short-lived, canceled the next year because of a lack of articles. Ironically, the Little Hoosier magazine of student writings, *Notes on Indiana,* begun in 1967, flourished. Eventually it ceased publication for the opposite reason: too many student contributions.

Between 1968 and 1982 school clubs competed in cemetery records searches. The Colonial Dames of Indiana awarded two cash prizes annually to the clubs that submitted the greatest number of accurate records.[2] The IJHS worked with the Genealogy Division of the Indiana State Library that located, by county, cemeteries for which there were no records. Tombstone inscription data collected by clubs throughout the state were added to the library's genealogical collection.

Like most other IJHS projects, the cemetery surveys taught both history and useful research skills.[3] During the 1968–69 school year, IJHS clubs submitted twenty thousand tombstone records to the Indiana State Library, according to the *National Junior Historian Newsletter.*

The best stimulation for clubs came at the workshops for officers and sponsors in the fall and the annual convention for all members in the spring. Under the constitution adopted in 1962, the elected state officers made most of the decisions concerning the IJHS program for the upcoming year, including planning and conducting state meetings. Montgomery might nudge them in a certain direction, but he wanted them to have a voice. Speaking before groups and conducting meetings not only honed the leadership skills of the officers but also gave them confi-

dence. The conventions and, to a lesser degree, the conferences served a wider purpose by fostering competition among the separate clubs, which, in turn, encouraged greater local participation.

One workshop in particular from which state officers could profit was Kentuckiana, a joint annual meeting with the state officers of the Kentucky Young Historians. The two groups first met in August 1967 at Rough River, Kentucky, and formed what became a long association. From then on the joint state junior societies' meeting alternated, with Indiana hosting in the even-numbered years. It was a broadening leadership experience for the officers of both groups, offering the chance to exchange ideas and to plan their respective fall workshops.[4]

Two-day IJHS fall workshops for officers and sponsors were conducted at state parks, in the early years at McCormick's Creek, and then, from 1966, at Spring Mill. The limited number of rooms at the parks' inns restricted the number attending to four officers or delegates and two sponsors from each club. True to Montgomery's philosophy, students conducted the workshops, with the executive committee and the state officers and directors leading the sessions.

The meeting format was similar each year. After a greeting from the president and a backward look at the IJHS by another officer, the two divisions, junior and senior, separated for meetings on membership, fund-raising, and club projects. For the general meetings Montgomery or a special guest spoke, usually on a historical topic. Saturday night entertainment usually consisted of club skits and folksinging; members departed on Sunday after a devo-

North Central club, 1964. *Indianapolis Star Magazine*

(Top) School 82 at the 1968 convention. *Indiana Historical Bureau*

(Bottom) Keith Shallenberger and Leslie Archer campaign material. *Indiana Historical Bureau*

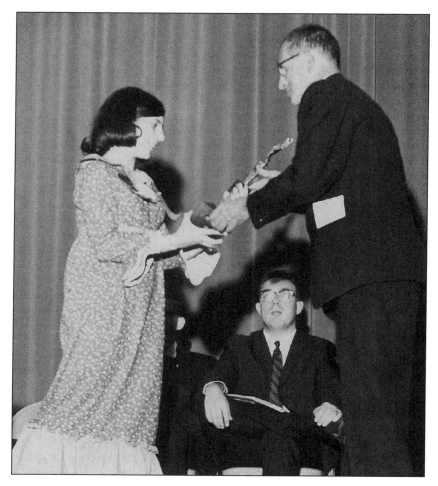

Bob Montgomery presents the Director's Trophy to School 82 at the
1968 convention. *Indiana Historical Bureau*

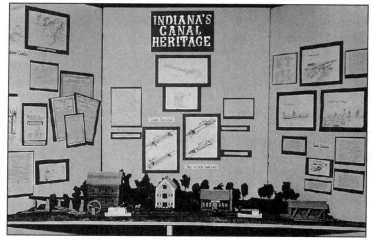

(Top) Convention exhibit, 1966. *Indiana Historical Bureau*

(Bottom) 1968 convention exhibit. *Indiana Historical Bureau*

Mrs. Samuel Harrel presents the award for Outstanding Club at the 1963 convention. *Indiana Historical Bureau*

(Top, left) Al Hodge awards the Governor's Cup at the 1968 convention. *Indiana Historical Bureau*

(Top, center) Mike Westfall presents the Bessie Keeran Roberts Award to Kathleen Landis in 1968. *Indiana Historical Bureau*

(Top, right) Al Hodge presents the Franklin County Traveling Trophy to Rossville in 1968. *Indiana Historical Bureau*

(Bottom) Award winners at the 1964 convention. *Indiana Historical Bureau*

tional service.[5] A similar annual workshop for Little Hoosier officers and sponsors was initiated in 1972.

The annual spring conventions took place in late April or early May in the tradition of the 1938 meeting at Marion. Open to all members, activities included the election of state officers and directors, the display of the local clubs' exhibits, and the presentation of awards.

In the Montgomery years the junior-senior state conventions were held at colleges or high schools in the Indianapolis area, central to clubs from all parts of the state. The host school, chosen at least a year in advance, was responsible for the luncheon and building arrangements. The IJHS executive committee drew up the agenda. Traditionally, the principal of the host school gave the welcome.[6]

Election of the new state officers and directors was of foremost interest, particularly in hotly contested races. Members of clubs that regularly participated in state projects and attended all-state meetings were already well acquainted. Many of these students were holding offices or serving on committees. Others, usually younger members caught up in the election activity, anticipated their own chances for state office. Holding an office in the local club was a good beginning, especially if the club had been recognized for good work.

Montgomery believed that the juniors should know they were appreciated. He also knew that competition was a stimulus. Over the years new contests were announced and new awards were given. He offered Certificates of Merit whenever possible. The more winners he could have, the more credit he could give to all who competed.[7]

The award for the outstanding club evoked the most interest. Until 1967 the senior trophy was given by the Indiana chapter of the National Society of Colonial Dames. Beginning in 1968 the highest honor in the senior division was the Governor's Cup, which was held by the recipient school for a year following its presentation.

The top club in the junior division received the Franklin County Traveling Trophy. Impartial judges, at first three and later five, made their choices after reviewing the annual reports the clubs submitted. Certificates of Merit rewarded the runners-up.

Other club awards included the Director's Trophy, which went to the school promoting the most new clubs, and the Attendance Trophy, which recognized the club with the largest number of members at the convention. A Club Award was given to the school that showed the greatest activities for five or more years. Each club was encouraged to take an exhibit to the convention, the only subject restriction being that it relate to Indiana history, and trophies were given for the best exhibits.[8]

The many exhibits on display at the convention gave impressive testimony of club activities. Topics included local industries, genealogy, minerals and fossils, folklore, famous Hoosiers, and pioneer crafts. Subjects were limited only by the ingenuity of a club's members.

Individuals also received recognition. The Farnham Scholarship, presented yearly by the Indiana Historical Society, provided a monetary gift to a graduating senior planning to attend an Indiana college; the award recognized the senior who in that year had contributed most to

Eli Lilly. *IHS*

(Top) The 1969 "History on Wheels" tour took Little Hoosiers on a weeklong bicycle and camping trip through southern Indiana. *Indiana Historical Bureau*

(Bottom) Participants in the infamous "History on Wheels" bicycle tour. Adult supervisors pictured are Bob Montgomery (top left), Nancy Lennox (standing below Montgomery), Dwight Taylor and Juanita Nelson (both seated below Lennox). *Indiana Historical Bureau*

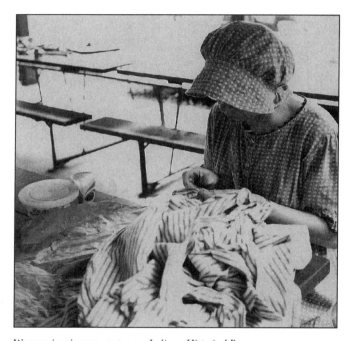

(Top and bottom left) Little Hoosier Camp, Muscatatuck Park.
Indiana Historical Bureau

(Bottom, right) Boy cooking over campfire. *Indiana Historical Bureau*

Woman in pioneer costume. *Indiana Historical Bureau*

Historians for the Future

the improvement of the IJHS.[9] The John H. Holliday Award, established in 1971 by the Society of Indiana Pioneers in honor of its first president, awarded fifty dollars, later one hundred dollars, to a graduating senior who, in the judgment of the director, had made an outstanding contribution to the IJHS.[10] That award, too, was to be used toward college. The Meritorious Service Awards went to members who had offered the greatest service to their clubs. For contributors of the best historical articles published in the IJHS magazine, *Hoosier Historian,* there were five awards.

Students received a number of other special awards. Two in particular deserve mention. The state chapter of the National Society of Colonial Dames was a longtime supporter of the IJHS. When the IJHS was struggling in the postwar period, the Colonial Dames contributed the first trophy for the outstanding club. Later they presented a sum of money annually toward the college expenses of the high school senior in the IJHS who was the most valuable contributor to the cemetery surveys, a special interest of the Colonial Dames.[11]

The Bessie Keeran Roberts Award was established in 1967 by the Allen County–Fort Wayne Historical Society to recognize an IJHS member who had written an outstanding paper on local history.[12] Contest entries described little-known facts in the county in which a member resided or in which his or her club was located. The award consisted of a traveling trophy, held by the club of the individual winner. Roberts, a Fort Wayne newspaperwoman, author, and historian, was very much interested in Indiana history and "in arousing the enthusiasm of young persons to learn about Indiana's past."[13]

Another award created in 1967 was the Little Hoosier Leadership Award for the senior or junior division club that most actively promoted the participation of Little Hoosier Historians.[14]

For all the motivation that Montgomery or anyone outside a club could give, the sponsor was the key to each club's vitality and longevity. Many sponsors came into the organization because of a personal contact with Montgomery. Al Hodge, who later developed a successful history club at Rushville, met the director one summer at an Indiana history class at Vincennes University. Montgomery had come to the class to line up IJHS sponsors. Hodge, after graduation from DePauw University, went to work for Montgomery in the summer of 1965 as a field agent.[15]

Other sponsors were teachers assigned by their principals to be club advisers or were already sponsors of school history clubs at the time of affiliation with the IJHS. For some teachers the first encounter with the IJHS was a workshop on Indiana history or a tour of historic sites. Sponsors helped Montgomery when he needed chaperones, camp counselors and instructors, and drivers with cars.

Eli Lilly, philanthropist and supporter of the Indiana Historical Society, praised Ruth Lawson for a detailed map her junior historians had made and displayed at the Indiana State Museum in 1972. "You are certainly doing a marvelous piece of work in teaching Indiana history to your children. It is to be hoped that the same good work is tak-

Robert Kirby used his experience as a history club sponsor when he became assistant director of the IJHS. *Indiana Historical Bureau*

(Top, left) Kirby with cap and sunglasses, camp 1986. *Indiana Historical Bureau*
(Top, right) Debbie Turpin as a student at Knightstown High School. *Indiana Historical Bureau*

(Bottom) Debbie Turpin Fausset with campers, 1980. *Indiana Historical Bureau*

ing place all over the state," wrote Lilly, who also complimented the children's handwriting. He added kind words for the IJHS director: "I suspect the fine hand of Mr. Robert Montgomery for he is certainly stirring up our children at the age where their memories will carry them throughout life."[16]

The early success of the Little Hoosier Historians school-year programs in the mid-1960s prompted IJHS leaders to consider the organization of more summer activities for the younger age group. Plans to offer a summer camp in 1967 were not realized, nor were hopes fulfilled for the first Little Hoosier Historian History Camp at Tippecanoe River State Park in July 1968.

A one-of-a-kind summer bicycle tour, which Montgomery dubbed "History on Wheels," took place in 1969. On a Sunday in July sixty grade-schoolers and their adult supervisors, with bicycles and camping gear, left Vincennes for a weeklong trip through parts of southern Indiana planned by Patricia Denker.

From Vincennes the group traveled to Petersburg, Jasper, the Lincoln State Park, and Rockport. The tour was not made solely by bicycle; the youngsters were transported to each new starting place by bus and were given a police escort through towns. They slept on porches and on the ground at Lincoln Village. Local historical societies and 4-H clubs along the way furnished meals; in Ferdinand, they were guests at a German picnic supper. Although the people they met along the route were helpful, there were difficulties—straying bicyclists, rain and flooding, and flat tires.

Montgomery was quick to rename the tour "Hell on Wheels." It was a great adventure for the youngsters, but it was not repeated. Montgomery realized the risks in this type of venture. During the next two summers Little Hoosiers traveled to southern Indiana on three-day bus tours, usually with three or four adults and several junior-senior division members as chaperones.[17] At night they slept out in the open.

On the last night of the 1971 bus tour the group slept inside on bunks at an old Boy Scout camp known as Muscatatuck in Jennings County. The facilities were primitive, but adequate. After the boys and girls were down for the night, the adults discussed how the IJHS might make use of the campsite. The result of the nocturnal brainstorming session was a detailed plan to establish the Little Hoosier pioneer camp in the summer of 1972. After gaining the approval of Hubert Hawkins and permission for using the campsite, the IJHS leadership began organizing the Little Hoosier Pioneer Arts and Crafts Camp. While the young campers were discovering skills and crafts of the early Indiana settlers, Montgomery made sure they learned something of the folklore and history of the Indiana frontier.[18]

When the Little Hoosier Historian division was organized in 1966, its conventions were patterned after the annual spring meeting of the older group. Like the junior-seniors, Little Hoosiers enjoyed competition. Trophies and plaques were given to chapters for the largest total membership and for the largest membership in attendance at the convention. The Outstanding Club Trophy and the Director's Award for recruiting new clubs were also presented. Trophies were given for the best exhibits, and cash prizes were awarded for the best examples of individual writing, and later, for artwork.

* * * *

Prior to 1972 the IJHS had to look to outside sources for funds, and many local historical groups, private businesses, and individuals responded to the solicitations of Hawkins, Montgomery, and others for funds to finance the summer programs of the IJHS. The Society of Indiana Pioneers contributed to the Wabash and Cass County architectural surveys, the Southeastern Indiana Water Crossing survey, and the dig at Fort Knox II.

The workshop at Homer was funded by the festival. The Rush County Historical Society helped underwrite the publication of the first Rush County study in exchange for several hundred free copies. The Vernon survey and booklet were supported by a number of individuals and business firms from the area as well as two Indianapolis architectural firms.[19]

When the Wabash city and county survey was planned, Montgomery approached the Honeywell Foundation at Wabash. The proposed cost was $1,165 to cover lodging and meals for seven days, film, transportation, and advance planning and publication expenses.[20] Most of the printing costs were covered by the Bureau and the Society. The Society of Indiana Pioneers assisted the IJHS with the survey in that county as did the Wabash County Historical Society, Honeywell, the Ford Meter Box Company, the *Wabash Plain Dealer,* and individuals in Wabash.[21] The financial aid was necessary; the goodwill and cooperation were also beneficial.

In 1972, through the efforts of Hawkins, the IJHS received a generous thirty thousand dollar grant from the Lilly Endowment. This welcome source of new income, set up to span three years, ended in 1976, but the IJHS was able to expand its programs and strengthen its leadership with additions to the staff.[22]

The IJHS was an acknowledged success by 1972. Throughout the country, however, the junior historical movement lost some of its popularity in the early 1970s; in some states the loss of members was much greater than it was in Indiana. Leaders believed that the IJHS summer program was the reason Indiana was retaining more members than other states.[23]

Montgomery had achieved no small amount of recognition and prestige for himself and the IJHS with his article, "History for Young People: Organizing a Junior Society," published as Technical Leaflet, No. 44, by the American Association for State and Local History (AASLH). Featured in the September 1967 issue of *History News,* the official publication of the AASLH, it was revised and reissued in 1972.

Also in 1972 the AASLH recognized the groundbreaking work of IJHS founder and Indiana Historical Society trustee Richard S. Simons of Marion, who had remained active in historical programs both at the state level and in Grant County. In the Award of Merit, Simons was lauded for his "pioneer efforts in organizing junior historical societies and for significant and long-sustained articles covering varied facets of Indiana's history and heritage."[24]

By 1973 the IJHS had a staff of five part-time employees

Jay Wilson, 1976. *Indiana Historical Bureau*

Bob Montgomery and students edit a tristate architectural survey on the dining room table at Conklin House.
Indiana Historical Bureau

in addition to Montgomery: Robert Kirby, a history club sponsor at School 82 in Indianapolis, was assistant director; Debbie Turpin, formerly a very active IJHS member, was administrative assistant; and three teacher-sponsors, Donna Jewel, Susie Weaver, and Jay Wilson, were acting field representatives.

One-fourth of Montgomery's time was devoted to administrative duties. As part of his job he reported to the agencies that sponsored the IJHS and corresponded with the more than two hundred clubs. He gave a certain number of hours monthly for editing and writing the IJHS newsletter and other publications. He was aware of the value of contact with other associations and individuals who supported the IJHS. He spent the bulk of his time, however, devoted to what he most enjoyed—direct involvement with the clubs and their members.[25]

At the end of 1973 Montgomery, tired and in ill health, retired as IJHS director. In January 1974 Robert Kirby, his handpicked successor, was named director. For another two years Montgomery sponsored the Whitewater Valley club with his wife Pauline and served as a consultant, particularly on state-sponsored architectural projects.

Robert Montgomery died on 17 June 1978. His colleagues recalled with great respect and affection his relentless efforts to build the Indiana Junior Historical Society. Thomas K. Krasean remembered the inexhaustible Montgomery as a man who gave thousands of juniors a better understanding of the past and a chance to be better citizens. "Bob would seek out clubs in every corner of the state (although as a southern-born Hoosier his car did seem to go in that direction more than any other)," he said. "Trying to keep up with Bob, as I did one summer on the Juniors' Ohio River trip, took endurance beyond the call of duty."[26]

One of those juniors paid tribute to Montgomery's vast knowledge of history and great love for young people. "I can recall him saying, 'Too many old folks just sit around and gripe about politics and the younger generation. They don't believe there are any good kids left,'" said Jon Turpin. "Mr. Montgomery was always ready to speak up for the young people and make sure that they received recognition when it was due."[27]

Hubert Hawkins had seen his confidence in Montgomery confirmed tenfold. "Under Bob's guidance Indiana developed the best junior history program in the nation. He received national recognition for his work," said Hawkins in the eulogy for his colleague and friend. "In a very real sense this vigorous organization, the IJHS, is a monument to Bob. It was the monument he would have chosen."[28]

CHAPTER 5

Sustaining IJHS Beyond the Seventies

When Robert Kirby succeeded Robert Montgomery as director of the Indiana Junior Historical Society, he inherited a strong network of history clubs and a variety of established statewide programs, but he faced challenges that included busing and the decline of neighborhood schools, changes in high school curricula and scheduling, and student after-school employment, which affected many high school extracurricular activities.[1]

Although there is little evidence in the Kirby era of the political activism so noteworthy in the IJHS under Montgomery's direction in the 1960s, the state legislature congratulated the IJHS for its services and achievements during the first regular session of the 99th General Assembly in 1975. House Concurrent Resolution No. 23 recognized the involvement of more than ten thousand young Hoosiers, the architectural surveys, the Goddard School restoration, and the juniors' work on the Lockport property. In Section 2 of the resolution the General Assembly recommended that "each Indiana school principal give careful and serious consideration to the advantages of establishing a chapter of the Indiana Junior Historical Society in his or her school."[2]

Despite the legislators' encouragement, stimulating sponsors and students in the high school clubs became more difficult as IJHS membership fell. Some sponsors had little or no contact with club members except at meetings. Unlike the elementary schools, in which Indiana history was still taught in fourth grade as a result of curriculum reforms in the 1960s, high schools rarely offered courses about the state's heritage. It appeared that the fears of the IJHS members who argued unsuccessfully for a required Indiana history high school course in the 1960s were realized in the 1970s and 1980s.

Over time the number of junior-senior clubs in the IJHS slowly decreased and the number of Little Hoosier chapters multiplied. In 1972, for example, there were 52 Little Hoosier chapters and 144 junior-senior clubs.[3] By the 1986–87 school year, there were 117 Little Hoosier chapters serving 5,975 students and 35 junior-senior division clubs serving 770 students.[4] The number of Little Hoosier chapters more than doubled, while the number of junior-senior clubs dropped by more than 75 percent.

Recruiting new clubs to the IJHS was relatively easy at the lower grades because teachers needed materials on the state's history. The IJHS workshops for elementary teachers continued to bring in new chapters. One reason for the workshops' popularity was the variety of presentations. Sponsors described crafts, projects, and techniques that could be adapted for classroom use. "They were wonderful meetings," said retired sponsor Marjorie Snodgrass. "They gave us time to share ideas and projects, and I learned a great deal."[5]

As the number of Little Hoosier sponsors increased, so did the number of talented presenters available for workshop sessions. With the Elementary Teachers Workshops conducted in northern and southern Indiana in alternate years, the IJHS could reach 250 teachers in a year's time. Even teachers who were not Little Hoosier sponsors could further the IJHS goal of making more Indiana youngsters aware of their state's history.[6]

In 1978 Kirby reinstated a Teachers' Tour of Historic Southwestern Indiana. Montgomery had conducted similar tours in the 1960s. The teachers on the 1978 pilgrimage, traveling by chartered bus, toured Vincennes, New Harmony, Angel Mounds, and the Lincoln Boyhood National Memorial. They stayed at Vincennes University and had meetings at the Lewis Library there.[7]

A later IJHS-teacher activity, planned for 1982, was a summer camp for teachers only. The proposed curriculum was to duplicate the Little Hoosiers summer camp program: crafts, pioneer skills, nature study, dancing, a Civil War encampment, using local records, and archaeology. Evidently teachers preferred the one-day workshop because the response to the adult summer camp was unenthusiastic.[8]

The success of the Little Hoosier Pioneer Arts and Crafts Camp at Muscatatuck Park from the summer of 1972 forward increased the popularity of the Little Hoosier program for students. Campers not only learned history and handicrafts but also good manners and fair play. From the early morning flag raising to lights-out, participants adhered to the camp routine.[9] College students staffed the kitchen, and counselors were fifteen- and sixteen-year-old junior-senior division members. The adults, in addition to Kirby and his assistants, were mainly IJHS sponsors.

Eighty Little Hoosiers signed up for the first camp session at Muscatatuck in 1972. In subsequent years the number of campers increased, and there was always a waiting list. A second week was added in 1980 and a third in 1984. Even the extra week, however, failed to accommodate every hopeful camper. Marjorie Snodgrass, who sponsored a Little Hoosier club at Indianapolis Public School 110 from 1984 to 1989, said that not one of her charges ever made the camp enrollment cut in four years.[10]

In the first years the staff and campers pretended it was just before or just after statehood for Indiana. Some participants were Indians and some were pioneers coming through Indiana on their way west. The two groups lived together for a week and learned each other's ways. In their classes campers were taught Indian as well as pioneer crafts. On the final night of camp there was a celebration—a going-away party for the pioneer family moving on.[11]

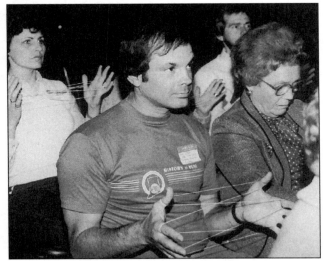

(Top, left) Girl in pioneer dress. *Indiana Historical Bureau*
(Top, right) Folk dancing. *Indiana Historical Bureau*

(Bottom) At IJHS workshops for elementary teachers, sponsors described crafts, techniques, and projects that could be adapted for classroom use. *Indiana Historical Bureau*

Kevin Stonerock as a trapper (in costume) with campers. *Indiana Historical Bureau*

Dwight Taylor with drums. *Indiana Historical Bureau*

Evelyn Howell, Dwight Taylor, and Candy Taff Carr. *Indiana Historical Bureau*

Historians for the Future

Through the years camp formats changed, but the focus remained the same. Classes fell into four categories: pioneer skills such as blacksmithing, sheep shearing, and candle dipping; early crafts such as cross-stitching and tole painting; pioneer entertainment such as square dancing and folk music; and outdoor life as in wilderness survival or tracking or living with nature. New classes were added each year.

Dwight Taylor and Glen Dillman created Everyday Life classes in which campers used the two fireplaces in the stone cabin. Led by costumed instructors, campers became caught up in an unwritten script about a family of the era involved in planned events that seemed to happen spontaneously. Costumes and events, even tools and equipment, were true to the historical period. Campers participated in pioneer weddings and funerals and even, on occasion, in a mock Civil War battle. Another time the theme shifted from pioneers to Indians, and there were classes in Indian dancing, Indian cooking, beadwork, and weaponry.[12]

Living history remained part of the camp program. Evelyn Howell later joined Taylor and Dillman, and the three cast themselves as Squire Dillman, Grandpa, and Auntie Howie.[13] Camp staff members, particularly Dillman and Jay Wilson, used living history with considerable success in their classrooms. Marlene Burns developed two fur trader roles, a white woman named Granny and an Indian called She-she-bens.[14] Campers who dressed as pioneers for Friday night's square dancing and folk songs were caught up in living history.

The camp week ran from Sunday to Saturday. From Monday through Thursday campers followed a schedule of morning and afternoon classes with a recreation period before dinner. Skits were the usual evening entertainment. The schedule changed on the final full day of camp. Miniclasses were offered to give boys and girls a chance to learn a new craft or skill. In some years special pioneer activities and games were organized.

Strong friendships formed among the Little Hoosiers, especially those who returned to camp for a second or third year. Many campers returned later as cooks' helpers and counselors. A camaraderie developed, too, among members of the adult staff. The turnover was small. Teachers looked forward to camp as eagerly as any of the young campers.

Especially important to the camp's success was the interaction of the three age groups. The high school students, addressed by their surnames, directed their squads and were responsible for the campers' behavior. The adult instructors interacted with the older IJHS members, guiding them in carrying out the camp program.

Planning for the following summer, camper Kathy Koontz wrote to Kirby in October 1978. While her spelling might have been irregular, her enthusiasm was genuine.

Dear Mr. Kerby,

I went to Little Hooshier Camp this year and I really enjoyed it, and I was wondering if you could send me some forms for Little Hooshier Camp so I could go to camp as a indavisable [individual] member. Since are chapter doesn't have Little Hooshiers in the sixth grade.[15]

As the number of Little Hoosier chapters grew, participation at conventions increased. In 1986, for example, 806 Little Hoosiers attended the meeting in Hope, accompanied by 66 sponsors and 100 visitors. Forty-one chapters were represented.[16] School groups that traveled long distances to the convention site often stayed overnight at the host school, where students arranged arts and crafts demonstrations, games and other group activities, or a swim in the high school pool.[17]

The American Association for State and Local History (AASLH) presented the Stalker Little Hoosiers of Bedford, Indiana, led by Jay Wilson, an Award of Commendation in 1979. Among many other activities, the chapter compiled a remarkable booklet about Revolutionary War soldiers buried in Lawrence County. In most cases students used photostatic copies of the veterans' benefit papers from the National Archives in Washington, D.C. The booklet included photographs of the gravestones and a simplified map showing the cemeteries.[18]

The Wabash Middle School History Club, sponsored by Ron Woodward, received a Certificate of Commendation in 1981 from the AASLH for its publications and promotion of local history.[19]

With Kirby's encouragement, a loyal group of dedicated teachers continued to promote the history clubs in junior high and high schools, chaperoning history tours, digs, and surveys. Their clubs were active at workshops and conventions. The IJHS summer programs for juniors and seniors also contributed to keeping club members interested. Most of the IJHS state activities established during Montgomery's era continued when Kirby became director.

History tours continued to be a part of the summer program. Perhaps Kirby's most creative summer adventure was the 1976 retracing of the route of Confederate general John Hunt Morgan and his raiders through southern Kentucky, Indiana, and Ohio. Connersville sponsor Harry Smith gave Kirby the idea after Smith and several students took a similar trip to collect material about Morgan's Raiders for the club's state convention project. Smith, Kirby, Glen Dillman, and two adults from Kentucky accompanied thirteen students on the excursion.

In 1863, when John Hunt Morgan and his men crossed the Ohio River and swept through Indiana and Ohio, they brought the Civil War very close to home. More than one hundred years later, the juniors group began their trip at Burkesville, Kentucky, on the Cumberland River and moved north to Bardstown, Kentucky, and on to Corydon and Batesville in Indiana. From there they traveled to Pomeroy, Ohio, on the Ohio River and then up to Lisbon in northeastern Ohio, where Morgan was captured in 1863. In the three states the young historians talked with local citizens and collected stories about horse thieving, looting, and the other escapades of Morgan's men. This project is one of the few that was completed without a booklet.[20]

Other popular summer trips were to southwestern Indiana, Vincennes, and to northeastern Indiana. Basically the same patterns were followed, but there were occasional changes in the itineraries and arrangements. A trip from Indianapolis to Fort Wayne in 1978 varied from the direct route, beginning with a visit to Battle Ground, near La-fayette, and including a stop in Crawfordsville to see Lane Place, the Gen. Lew Wallace Study, and the Old Jail Museum.[21] In 1982 twenty students and four adults touring northern Indiana stayed in college dormitories at North Manchester.[22] In 1987 a small group touring southern Indiana by car stopped at Spring Mill, Spencer, and Jeffersonville and made an architectural tour of New Albany.[23]

High school students from five history clubs participated in an oral history project at Leavenworth in the summer of 1983. The Crawford County town was washed out in a 1937 flood and was later rebuilt on higher ground. Kirby and his staff were uncertain about just how to research the flood and its effects, so they announced the proposed study as a "mystery project." Working with a local historian, IJHS members talked with a number of county residents who recalled the flood. The residents described the flood itself, their reactions to relocations, and problems and solutions. Students also explored the locale's architecture and conducted local records research.[24]

As cemetery searches continued, the IJHS published a booklet in 1973 describing Henry County cemetery inscriptions and epitaphs, and another in 1976 dealing with cemetery folk art in the Whitewater valley.

Teams went out on architectural surveys through 1979, exceeding Montgomery's ten-year plan. The John Conner Junior Historical Society compiled the material for *Laurel, A Hoosier Community,* which the IJHS published in 1975. In Lawrence County a Little Hoosier Historians chapter put together a booklet titled *One Hundred Years of Lawrence County, Indiana, Architecture,* published in 1976 by the IJHS.

In 1976 a team from several communities examined both historical and modern buildings in Versailles, a small southeastern Indiana community settled in 1818. Earlier studies in other communities had focused on nineteenth-century buildings. By 1976, however, "the projects could no longer offer new subjects to the students, and a departure was made from studying only nineteenth-century architecture," according to the introduction to *Versailles, A Small Indiana Town, 1818–1976,* published in 1980.

In Versailles, a government housing project built when the Jefferson Proving Grounds opened in 1941 affected subsequent residential and commercial construction. "Since then the town has had a steady, if not rapid, growth, represented by subdivisions and modern ranch-style homes. 'Highway rash' has erupted on U.S. 421 on the south edge of town," wrote the students in the booklet's introduction. They criticized the government housing project for the courteous but indifferent treatment accorded to the IJHS group by Versailles citizens during their research visit. Bob Montgomery assisted on the Versailles survey.

In 1980 the AASLH recognized the IJHS with an Award of Merit for "developing a statewide program to survey Indiana's architectural heritage."[25] Bob Montgomery's ideas and programs continued to draw attention and accolades to Indiana.

With Kentucky Junior Historians, IJHS members continued the joint architectural studies on several bistate projects. Students surveyed Carroll, Washington, and Madison

Counties in both Indiana and Kentucky in 1975 and 1976. In June 1977 twelve IJHS students and five adults made a survey of architecture in Franklin County, Indiana, and in 1979 a similar number visited Steuben County for the last of the IJHS surveys.[26]

In 1975 Kirby introduced the Muscatatuck Summer History Workshop, a new, weeklong activity for junior-senior members, which eventually replaced the architectural surveys. The workshops, conducted at the Muscatatuck Jennings County Park campground, were intended to involve more people and to improve the overall program of the IJHS. Classes were offered in the techniques of historical study: genealogy, local records research, folklore, oral history, archaeology, and architecture. The participants used the Jennings County Courthouse and nearby cemeteries as resources and practiced archaeological skills at Tunnel Mill and other locations nearby. Like the Little Hoosiers in their stay at Muscatatuck, the junior-senior members slept in converted quail hatcheries, ate in the dining hall, and organized evening entertainment.

The workshop curriculum changed in 1980 when basketry was added. The next year, by request, other craft classes were offered: quilting, knife making, card loom weaving, and woodworking. In time the format was changed to include a greater number of classes of shorter duration. Local records research and archaeology and architecture became less popular, while more emphasis was placed on pioneer skills. In the first years workshop attendance was limited to twenty-five. Enrollment by the late 1980s had more than doubled.[27] This workshop became an impor-

tant training ground for counselors for the Little Hoosier camps.

Getting the campground at Muscatatuck in good order for the Little Hoosier camp and the Summer Workshop became a concern to Kirby and his staff, who scheduled the first Muscatatuck Work Camp in 1978. Student volunteers in the first year built picnic tables and cleaned dorms. Later projects called for volunteers to clean the kitchen and dormitories, put the grounds in order, and practice their skills with hammer and paint brush. The IJHS made substantial improvements and contributed to the upkeep of this county facility in order to use it for programs.

Archaeological projects had certain advantages over architectural surveys as summer IJHS activities. More students could be included, and daily transportation involved less driving. Participants used archaeology as a means of learning about people and their culture.

Marcy Gray directed a dig in 1973 at Oakland Farm, which had belonged to Solomon Meredith, a general in the Civil War.[28] The property was located on the southern edge of Cambridge City. The juniors expected to locate four buildings that were no longer standing during the dig at the Meredith farm. They set up a grid and made excavations at the site of a carriage house or stable.

In 1974 Gray, by then an anthropology major at Indiana University, led nineteen IJHS members and five adults in an excavation project at the Fred Paxson farm north of Pennville in Jay County.[29] The goal at the Paxson farm was to locate the farmstead, which dated back to the mid-1800s. A second purpose of the project was to teach archaeological

Marlene Burns. *Indiana Historical Bureau*

(Top) Pioneer wedding.
Indiana Historical Bureau

(Bottom) A 1976 IJHS summer program traced Gen. John Hunt Morgan's raid through southern Kentucky, Ohio, and Indiana. Group in front of Morgan's Raid marker. *Indiana Historical Bureau*

(Top) Plaque from marker.
Indiana Historical Bureau

(Bottom) Historical marker in Indiana.
 Indiana Historical Bureau

Pauline Montgomery remained involved with the juniors long after the death of her husband Bob. Here, she attended the Muscatatuck Workshop in 1977. *Indiana Historical Bureau*

(Top) Oakland Farm dig, 1973. *Indiana Historical Bureau*

(Bottom) French House dig, 1980. *Indiana Historical Bureau*

Marcy Gray, Cammeck's Mill dig, 1975. *Indiana Historical Bureau*

Historians for the Future

techniques by showing students how to find artifacts and document them.

An exciting discovery at the Paxson farm turned out to be a hoax. Diggers unearthed a large flat stone that appeared to be a piece of fieldstone that would have been used as part of a farmhouse foundation. The crew took pictures and mapped the unit, taking care not to move the stone from where it was found. But one person took up the stone and discovered a message on it—written in magic marker. Gray did not appreciate the humor in a sponsor's practical joke. Regretting the loss of four work hours, she gave an on-the-spot lecture about taking archaeology seriously. Ironically, the rock was the only finding the crew was able to map.[30]

From an archaeologist's point of view, the 1975 dig at Cammeck's Mill in western Wayne County near the town of Milton was probably the most successful of the IJHS digs. The two-week activity permitted twice the number of IJHS members to take part as had the previous year's dig, and there was more time for investigating the selected site. Digging in the ground depression, the crews uncovered the edges of a cellar and low rows of foundation. They found many different domestic artifacts, now the property of Marcy Gray. Instead of the mill and the millrace, which they expected to find, they located the miller's house. Because the mill had been destroyed, probably in the 1860s or 1870s, the artifacts found there could be dated to the mid-nineteenth century.[31]

Twenty-five IJHS members explored another canal lock in 1976, the Milton lock on the Whitewater Canal in Wayne County. The dig uncovered the old wooden floor at the lower end, exposing the lock's triangular mechanism and revealing how it had been constructed and how it had operated more than a century earlier. Bob and Pauline Montgomery furnished historical background about this lock, the last one in the canal before Cambridge City. Some participants wished that the project could have lasted longer than one week.[32]

There were bistate digs as well. Supervised by James R. Jones III, a graduate archaeology student from Indiana University, two separate crews made up of young historians from Kentucky and Indiana met at Vincennes in June 1980 to participate in the French House dig. The crews, each one there a week, dug in the backyard of the old house.[33]

Also in the summer of 1980 thirteen IJHS members and eleven Kentucky juniors attended the Kampsville One-Week Archaeological Workshop conducted by the Northwestern University Archaeological Program at Kampsville, Illinois, 270 miles southwest of Chicago. Workshop instructors provided fieldwork, lectures and seminars, lab briefings, and field trips tailored to the interests and abilities of high school students. Classes were conducted in the evenings.[34]

Because of expanded IJHS summer projects and new summer programs within the KJHS, an exchange program evolved between the two junior societies. The last of the joint digs took place in June 1984 at Frankfort, Kentucky.[35] Four IJHS members joined an ongoing excavation of the Old Capitol Square in Frankfort supervised by Ron Deiss, a Murray State University historical archaeologist. The students learned how to open and map a site and how to catalog artifacts. Kirby and his staff determined that while working with the university crews offered some benefits, the dig would have been more beneficial if the IJHS members had been as skilled in archaeology as the college students and if they had received more guidance.[36]

In 1977 the IJHS showcased its efforts to interest young Hoosiers in their state and its history by taking part in the celebration of the 1977 centennial session of the Indiana General Assembly. IJHS members of all ages were asked to contribute miniature models depicting Indiana's legislative history. The exhibit in the statehouse rotunda opened on 21 March and continued until late in April. The displays depicted the development of canals, covered bridges, the common schools, the displacement of Native American tribes, and other topics.[37] For the next two years the IJHS participated in the Statehouse Exhibit, repeated because of its initial success. The IJHS staff decided that clubs would participate only in alternate years, during the long sessions of the General Assembly.[38]

The IJHS continued to work with its counterparts in other states to organize regional gatherings. The George Rogers Clark Symposium, cosponsored with the Kentucky Junior Historical Society and heralded in the *IJHS Newsletter* as "a great opportunity for IJHS members to show adults what young historians can do," took place from 19 to 21 June 1979 in Vincennes.[39] The occasion was the bicentennial of Clark's recapture of Fort Sackville at Vincennes. The meeting was open to all IJHS members as well as junior historical societies in other states. Representatives from nine states participated.[40]

At the core of the Clark symposium was an essay contest. Five winners, juniors or seniors in high school, represented five states in which George Rogers Clark played a pivotal historical role: Virginia, Pennsylvania, Kentucky, Illinois, and Indiana. These essays, based on research regarding Clark's activities in the students' respective states, were presented orally at the symposium. Although the projected publication of the papers did not materialize,[41] the symposium enlarged the scope of IJHS activities by drawing in junior organizations from several states.[42]

Junior historical clubs completed several significant restoration projects after the 1973–74 Goddard School restoration. A television film, viewed on WTTV's "At Home in Indiana" in 1977, captured a school day as it might have been in the late 1880s at the Goddard School. Joe Turpin, a former IJHS state officer, was the "schoolmaster" who "taught school" to modern-day students posing as his pupils.[43]

The 1985 restoration of Adams Mill near Cutler in Carroll County evolved from then fourteen-year-old Roy Ladd's enthusiasm for local history and the encouragement of Glen Dillman, his IJHS club sponsor. The original flour mill was built in 1831 by John Adams of Pennsylvania and operated for more than 110 years. After staging festivals at the mill in the 1970s, owner Jim Broadhurst of Valparaiso closed it and put it up for sale in 1979, but the property was not sold and remained abandoned. In 1985 Ladd persuaded his club, the Carroll Historians, that restoring the old flour mill would be an excellent project for the group. Students devoted more than three hundred hours of labor cleaning up

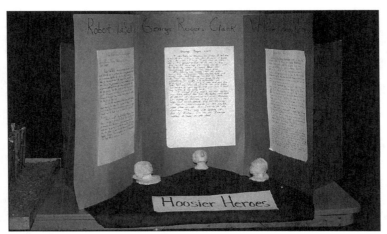

Statehouse Exhibit. *Indiana Historical Bureau*

Students from several states participated in the George Rogers Clark Symposium. *Indiana Historical Bureau*

(Top) Roy Ladd was the driving force behind the Carroll Historians' restoration of Adams Mill. *Glen Dillman*

(Bottom) The Huntington club received a national award for its efforts in restoring Chief Richardville's home. Left to right, James Biddle, president of the National Trust for Historic Preservation, and Jean Gernand, Charles Clark, and Mary Kelsay, Indiana Junior Historical Society sponsors. *Jean Gernand*

the building and grounds, repairing machines, and making the mill operable again. An estimated 150 members from 13 clubs gathered at Adams Mill on 15 September 1985 to see a working mill and craft demonstrations.[44]

IJHS clubs discovered many ways to share their activities with other groups. Genealogy workshops open to all IJHS clubs were sponsored for several years by the Whitewater Valley Junior Historical Society.[45] Later, the Wabash Junior High School history club invited other IJHS members to workshops designed for beginning genealogists.[46]

Pauline Montgomery's Whitewater Valley club sponsored motor tours that followed the Whitewater Canal from Cambridge City through Connersville and Laurel to Metamora and Brookville. Harry Smith's Connersville High School history club sponsored a train trip through the Whitewater Valley from Connersville to Metamora and back again. The big club project for the Connersville club for several years was its annual trek in late October to the Civil War battlefields of Gettysburg and Antietam and to Harpers Ferry and Fort Necessity. The seven state officers were invited to go along in 1977, and Kirby, Debbie Turpin Fausset, and Carl Zenor accompanied them. Two years later the state officers again accompanied the club on the trip.[47]

The Huntington North Junior Historical Society was one of three groups in the country to win the Young Preservationists Award of the National Trust for Historic Preservation in 1978. The Huntington club had restored the home of Jean Baptiste Richardville, one of the last prominent leaders of the Miami Nation of Indians. The Chief Richardville Home, a frame house at the outskirts of Huntington, was built in 1833 on land that had been deeded to Richardville's mother by a French official. Chief Richardville had moved the Indian capital in 1831 from Kekionga near Fort Wayne to the forks of the Wabash to escape the white man's civilization.[48] Representative John Brademas presented the award to members of the Huntington club at a Washington, D.C., ceremony in 1978.[49]

In 1982 the AASLH recognized the Rushville High School club for its oral history studies by bestowing an Award of Merit for the "use of oral history as a resource tool in the collection and preservation of the history of Rush County."[50]

Bob Kirby enhanced the student workshop concept he inherited from Bob Montgomery. The workshops Montgomery had arranged were generally planning meetings for officers and sponsors on both the state and local levels. The Kentuckiana, established in August 1967, brought together state officers of the Kentucky Junior Historical Society and the IJHS every summer, with Indiana hosting the meetings in alternate years. The annual Fall Workshop for junior-senior division officers and sponsors, in effect since 1960, offered leadership training for newly elected local club officers.

For a number of years the Indiana Historical Society's Spring Conference provided a few IJHS members the opportunity to participate in an adult historical workshop. Fellowships were awarded to four or five juniors, selected by application, and the IJHS was given a place on the program as a separate conference section. Frequently the IJHS used this opportunity to share special accomplishments with the adult history group.

At Kirby's direction, the IJHS introduced fall workshops open to all junior and senior members in 1975. Organized in response to club requests, these innovative one-day events took place at Conner Prairie Pioneer Settlement in Noblesville. Scheduled early in the school year—in September in the early years and, later, in mid-October—these workshops inspired the clubs at the beginning of a new school year. Attendance over the years was good with two hundred to three hundred club members and sponsors on hand each time, representing approximately twenty clubs.[51]

The fall Conner Prairie workshop was replaced in 1984 with a new activity, held at Stonycreek Farm, also in the Noblesville area north of Indianapolis. The IJHS Pioneer Festival at Stonycreek offered clubs an opportunity to showcase the crafts and skills of their members. Well in advance of each festival, IJHS state officers announced specific years as themes around which activities were to be organized. On one occasion the IJHS Alumni Association reenacted the 1840 presidential election when Martin Van Buren lost to William Henry Harrison. Another time the festival centered around the year 1856; another time, 1860. In 1988 the festival became a 1904 carnival with club booths offering games of chance and prizes to those people who held the most winning tickets. The Stonycreek festival ceased to be an exclusive junior-senior activity in 1988 when Little Hoosier chapters were invited to send representatives.[52]

In March 1982 the first of the Late Winter Workshops took place at the Indiana State Library and Historical Building in Indianapolis. The idea for this conference did not originate with Kirby. In fact, he was not altogether convinced of its merit. The Mary Bryan Pioneers, a Southport history club, had, with Kirby's permission, conducted a workshop for IJHS clubs at the State Library the previous March. They had asked for the late winter meeting because they thought it would be a good time to get together with IJHS friends who had not met since fall or, in some cases, since the last convention. Several sponsors endorsed the idea of an annual March workshop,[53] and thirteen clubs attended.[54]

With the convention competition only two months away, organizers hoped that the Late Winter Workshop would spur both clubs and individuals to work on their projects. A special feature of this workshop, which proved successful from the start, was club sponsorship. Each year a different junior-senior club volunteered to host the workshop. The 1986 meeting was planned by IJHS individual members, junior-senior students who were members of the state society but had no specific club affiliation.

The state convention continued to be the high point of the IJHS year. Even clubs that had not participated in any other IJHS event during the year prepared projects for the convention. For many clubs, completing a project was the major accomplishment of the year, some physical evidence of their efforts not only for them but also for all the other IJHS members and sponsors.[55]

Kirby also enjoyed rewarding as many IJHS members as possible for their various achievements. At spring conventions for both junior-seniors and Little Hoosiers, plaques were awarded to clubs with the largest membership, with the largest percentage of total membership in attendance,

Sponsor Glen Dillman was a reliable supporter of the pioneer festivals at Stonycreek Farm. *Indiana Historical Bureau*

(Top) "Box lunch" auction at Stonycreek Farm, 1988. *Indiana Historical Bureau*

(Bottom, left) Presentation of Outstanding Chapter Award, 1981. *Indiana Historical Bureau*
(Bottom, right) Debbie Turpin Fausset and Bob Kirby. *Indiana Historical Bureau*

and with the most years of continuous affiliation. Trophies honored winners for the best exhibits, by a club and by an individual. Over the years recognition was given for architectural surveys, cemetery records, oral history, and individual writing. Outstanding members were singled out to receive special awards.

The most valued prize, year after year, was the traveling trophy presented to the outstanding club or chapter, based on the year's achievements. Rivalries were strong, particularly among previous winners. New awards were added from time to time. The IJHS Alumni Association art contest for Little Hoosiers is one example. After Montgomery's death in 1978, the Director's Award was renamed the Bob Montgomery Memorial Award. It was given to the junior-senior or Little Hoosier club most successful in recruiting new clubs.

Competition for leadership positions was friendly but serious. School clubs wanted to put their candidates into a state office, and therefore campaigning became more sophisticated, with badges, posters, and even sandwich boards touting favorite candidates. Club members, friends from other schools, and candidates negotiated for votes.

With the grant of Lilly Endowment funds, the IJHS had the capacity to expand its staff in the late 1970s. The pressures of Kirby's job were considerably lessened in June 1977 when Debbie Turpin Fausset became a full-time assistant director.

Another young aide for Kirby was Kevin Stonerock, who joined the staff full time in October 1980 as a field representative. He, too, had become an IJHS member through the Knightstown club and first joined the program as an adult camp staff member teaching woodlore and square dancing. Little Hoosier Historian campers often recalled the staged pioneer wedding of Stonerock and the young woman to whom he was engaged. The youngsters were certain they had witnessed the real event.

Fausset and Stonerock assisted Kirby in producing programs of thirty to forty-five minutes, for IJHS clubs, which would comfortably fit into a school class period. Some were slide shows; others were narratives, often with music. Some, like "The IJHS—What Is It?" and "Spring Mill State Park," were promotional. Others explained such IJHS activities as "Morgan's Raid of 1863," "The Goddard School Restoration," and "Nineteenth Century Architecture." Others, with music, gave insight into people: "The Civil War in Song" and "Events in the Lives of Commonfolk." Still others were instructive: "Curing Meat in the Home," "Making Rawhide and a Dugout Canoe," and "Home Remedies," one for which Kirby was especially noted.[56]

Many changes awaited the IJHS in the late 1980s and early 1990s. One of the most significant was the retirement of Bob Kirby in 1987. His tenure had lasted thirteen years following Montgomery's nine years at the helm. The next two directors of the Indiana Junior Historical Society served less than two years apiece in a difficult period that tested the resiliency of the juniors, their sponsors, and the organization itself. A number of remarkable individuals, determined to sustain a young historians movement in Indiana and sometimes sharply at odds among themselves, found ways to strengthen the junior society that few of them probably would have predicted in the late 1980s.

CHAPTER 6

Leadership and Management Change at Fifty-Year Mark

Ten years before Robert Kirby retired as director of the Indiana Junior Historical Society in 1987, changes took place at the Indiana Historical Bureau and the Indiana Historical Society that had lasting implications for the management and programming of the juniors program.

When Hubert Hawkins, longtime Bureau director and Society executive secretary, retired in 1976, he was replaced by two distinguished professionals, Pamela J. Bennett to lead the Bureau and Gayle Thornbrough to direct the Society. This move represented the first time since the Bureau's creation as the Indiana Historical Commission in 1915 and as a permanent state agency in 1925 that the two organizations were not led by the same person.

Another event of far-reaching importance took place in 1977, when the Indiana Historical Society received a major bequest from longtime benefactor Eli Lilly consisting of "10 percent of his holdings in Eli Lilly Company, which amounted to 309,904 shares."[1] The gift boosted the Society's endowment from $3.6 million in 1976 to $22 million by 1979 and made it possible for the organization to enhance existing activities, initiate new projects, and hire more staff.[2]

In retrospect it seems easy to see that the 1974 retirement of Bob Montgomery, the 1976 departure of Hawkins, and the formal division of the Society and Bureau leadership in 1976 were destined to affect the IJHS. Both Bennett and Thornbrough had innovative plans for their respective organizations, and Montgomery's successor, Bob Kirby, was inclined to manage the juniors with considerable independence. Thus, the IJHS operated with little administrative oversight from either the Bureau or the Society until the late 1980s, although in May 1977 the Society board committed to funding the salary of a full-time assistant director for the IJHS, "freeing its director, Robert Kirby, to travel more around the state to promote the organization." The Society also provided increased financial support for the juniors' summer camps, workshops, and tours.[3]

In fulfilling the Bureau's mandated responsibilities, Bennett focused on educational outreach and building partnerships with other organizations in the state. The Bureau assumed responsibility for the Indiana program of the National History Day competition and allowed the IJHS to act as a district-at-large in the event beginning in 1982.[4] Since the Indiana contest was open to pupils from fourth through twelfth grades, both junior-senior clubs and Little Hoosier chapters could compete. The Bureau again became involved in the preparation of Indiana history curriculum materials. BROADSIDES, a curriculum supplement collection drawn from primary sources, was introduced in 1987. The Bureau began administration of the REACH program, an arts in education enterprise that takes museum-quality exhibits into schools, in 1988.

Thornbrough emphasized the Society's superb publications program. As a result of the Lilly bequest, the Society's Board of Trustees was able to expand a number of existing programs, including archaeological investigations of the Bean Blossom Creek drainage system and the Mann prehistoric site in Posey County. The Society also decided to sponsor an effort to record books for the blind in the fields of state and local history, extend outreach services to local historical societies and museums, make the research resources of its library more accessible to scholars, and develop new publications, including a study of Indiana newspapers, a new state guide to Indiana places of historic interest, and a newsletter informing Society members of Society activities.[5]

The IJHS continued to operate out of the Bureau offices after the Society moved in 1976 to the building addition on the west end of the Indiana State Library and Historical Building, funded by state allocations, the federal Library Service and Construction Act funds, and the gift from Eli Lilly. The Bureau covered some IJHS operating costs with appropriated funds from the state, which included the director's base salary. The Society, however, continued to underwrite most of the IJHS expenses, including the salaries for an office manager and a program coordinator, a position that was added in 1984.

In a 1990 memo, Thomas K. Krasean, the Society's community relations director and a steadfast supporter of IJHS activities since the 1960s, summarized the three stages of the juniors' development. "The first stage (1938–62) was one of sporadic growth, a mixture of ups and downs that did little more than keep the flame of interest alive," he said. "The second and perhaps the greatest stage (1962–89) began with the hiring of Robert Montgomery as the first full-time director. All of the extraordinary programs that made the IJHS one of the finest junior groups in the United States were developed under the guidance of Montgomery and the two men who eventually followed him: Robert Kirby and Kevin Stonerock. Stage three (1989) . . . will no doubt bring about some new developments in the IJHS."[6]

Gayle Thornbrough retired from the Society in 1984, and Peter T. Harstad was named to succeed her as executive director. Mindful of the Society's financial stake in the juniors' program, Harstad, with support from Bennett, hired Margaret A. Bonney from Iowa City, Iowa, in 1986 to review the operation and effectiveness of the IJHS. Specifically, Bonney's charge was "to evaluate the Indiana Junior Historical Society (IJHS) and its relationship to its spon-

Pam Bennett (left) welcomes actress Joanna Cassidy for the presentation of a Sagamore of the Wabash from Governor Evan Bayh. Miss Cassidy was in Indiana to film a documentary about Gene Stratton-Porter. She made a presentation to over 140 Little Hoosiers and sponsors at the fall leadership workshop in 1989. *Indiana Historical Bureau*

Gayle Thornbrough. *IHS*

soring organizations, including an assessment of organizational structure and program goals, cost effectiveness, printed materials, and activities; and to make recommendations concerning finances and content of the Indiana Junior Historical Society, both short and long range."[7]

Bonney based her evaluation on attendance at a teachers' workshop; interviews with sponsors, students, alumni, historians, and staff members; written materials provided by the Bureau and the Society; and research into junior historical organizations in other states.

In her report Bonney applauded the work of the IJHS and the ongoing support of the Bureau and the Society, stating that "among the 20 or so state level junior history club endeavors known to this reviewer, the Indiana program is quite possibly the best."[8]

However, she found the IJHS administrative structure to be "complicated and confusing," largely because of its finances. "Fiscal support for the IJHS comes from four sources: IHS, IHB, the State of Indiana by way of a grant, and a small IJHS working fund generated from dues and sales. Fiscal matters have in many cases simply evolved over a period of years into a situation of adequate support, inadequate documentation, and confused employees," Bonney stated.[9]

The grant to which Bonney referred was a $15,000 annual grant approved on 25 February 1976 by the General Assembly.[10] This represented the first state grant specifically for the IJHS, although the state had been funding the director's salary since 1965. The state allocation reinforced Bennett's intention to make the Bureau's services accessible to as many taxpayers as possible and the programs accountable to the public.

Programming, student involvement, volunteer support, and leadership in the IJHS received high marks from Bonney, who credited Kirby for running a "fine, nationally respected program." She applauded his rapport with young people, but pointed out that he had failed to submit "thorough yearly reports, especially fiscal reports."

Bonney also noted a "severe communication and credibility gap" in the operation of the IJHS. Bonney stated that "the fragmentation and confusion within the administrative and financial structure surely has contributed to this problem. The direct employment by the IHS of individuals working within the IJHS program has added to the confusion regarding lines of responsibility."[11]

Bonney recommended that the Indiana Historical Society continue its financial support of the IJHS, placing "as much fiscal control as possible with the Bureau director who will in turn report to the Society." She stated that the Bureau should integrate the various facets of its education program into a coherent department that would include the IJHS. Bonney added that the Bureau director would need to establish a "mandatory, well defined program for evaluation and fiscal accountability to which the Indiana Junior Historical Society director must adhere."[12]

In 1987 Bennett reorganized the Bureau's educational activities, creating an Education Division and placing the IJHS and other school-related programs under the supervision of an education director. Sheryl Vanderstel was the first individual to serve in that position. In January 1989

Vanderstel was succeeded by Virginia Terpening, an experienced educator from Baltimore, Maryland, who shared Bennett's desire to extend the reach of the Bureau's education programs and refused to be swayed by any arguments against change based on "We've always done it this way" reasoning.[13]

According to Krasean, the Bureau's creation of the new division initiated the third stage in the development of the IJHS. "The director of the IJHS now had to report to the new director of the division and some of the independent status, long held by the IJHS staff, was lost," he said.[14]

In a letter published in January 1988 and addressed to all IJHS members, Kirby announced his resignation: "There is really no need for me to make this a long letter because I can say what needs to be said very briefly. By the time you read this, I will no longer be the IJHS Director. Due to personal reasons I am retiring on December 28, 1987." He thanked past and present IJHS members for making enjoyable his years as director and asked the students to give his successors "the same cooperation that you have given me."[15] Kirby soon moved to Illinois where he remained until his death in 1994.

Bennett named Kevin Stonerock as Kirby's successor in 1988. Since the fall of 1984, when Debbie Turpin Fausset resigned, Stonerock had served as Kirby's assistant with the title of program coordinator. Brenda Houchins also joined the staff at that time to manage the office.[16]

In the newsletter that carried Kirby's resignation, Stonerock praised his predecessor as someone who cared about young people. "His goals for the IJHS have never been to flood the professional history ranks with former junior historians, but instead to instill a love for and a desire to learn about the past we share. In this, Mr. Kirby has succeeded," said Stonerock.[17]

History intrigued Stonerock, particularly the Civil War period, and he liked to teach youngsters nature lore, wilderness survival, and tracking. His greatest successes were at Muscatatuck, the Little Hoosier camp, and the summer workshop for older students. Several Stonerock observers believed he would have chosen to live in pioneer times if he had the choice. In the evenings at Muscatatuck when he played his guitar and sang folk songs, or when he taught campers the skills of tracking, he seemed to become a Hoosier pioneer.

Many IJHS members first came in contact with Stonerock when he appeared at their schools in the roles he adopted for his living history presentations. Stonerock's living history programs were designed to be educational, not simply entertaining. School visits were effective in reaching teachers of fourth, fifth, and sixth graders who were not yet affiliated with the Little Hoosier Historians.[18]

The pioneer trapper was the first character Stonerock developed. Andrew Ammonett, who had come into the Indiana Territory from Virginia by way of Kentucky, told about frontier life up to and during 1810. He talked about the Indians and showed his audience his weapons and other gear. Stonerock's next character was Billy Yank, William Fentress, who was billed as a "common Hoosier soldier for the Union." The experiences of Billy Yank—camp life, the food, the fighting—were believable to his listeners.

(Top) Dwight Taylor (left) and Tom Krasean.
Indiana Historical Bureau

(Bottom) Tom Krasean (left) and David Roberts. *IHS*

(Top) Peter T. Harstad. *IHS*

(Bottom) Virginia Terpening with juniors. *Indiana Historical Bureau*

They were impressed by his uniform and his rifle and other equipment. The third role was that of a Scottish fur trader of the late eighteenth century whose business was with both Indians and whites.

Stonerock was closer in age to the IJHS students than either of his predecessors. His enthusiasm for the program at Muscatatuck was contagious. By nature casual and low-key, Stonerock fostered a relaxed camp atmosphere. He was always cheerful and friendly, putting the youngsters at ease and disciplining gently. Stonerock's energy and creativity took over when he could team up with Jay Wilson or Glen Dillman to plan a new activity or play a practical joke on the campers and the staff.

In 1988, although the demand was still high, the Bureau cut one week of camp, offering only two one-week sessions because of staffing and scheduling difficulties.[19] The change was not popular with either longtime sponsors or Stonerock, and it was a portent of future changes. Liability issues, the need to reach larger numbers of children, and costs were among additional reasons for the cutback. Camp fees charged to participants had traditionally been kept low and rarely even covered the cost of food.

When Stonerock assumed the directorship he was involved in summer canoe trips initiated by sponsors. A Wabash River trip, planned in 1986 for twenty-two students and their adult leaders, was canceled because high water made the river too dangerous for canoeing. The group instead toured northern Indiana.[20] In 1987 a trip was set for the Tippecanoe River, a shallower but faster river. The canoe trip began at Rochester and ended at Leiters Ford, a trip of fifteen miles. After a day on the river the students traveled on land for the other two days, visiting the area's historic sites.[21]

The 1988 canoe trip on the upper waters of White River was more arduous. It began at Anderson as a motor trip and centered around eastern Indiana with visits to Mounds State Park and other points of interest in the Muncie area. With the river low because of drought—taking canoes twenty-five miles downriver from Daleville to Perkinsville required more time than the schedule allowed—the weary canoers were relieved to be back on land. One of the students, commenting that the students' trek was only a sample of what early settlers had to do routinely, was more appreciative of history. "It threw a different perspective onto my whole outlook of the settling of Indiana," he said.[22]

In mid-December 1988 the first annual IJHS Christmas Gathering took place when all junior-senior clubs were invited to a party given by the Carroll Historians in a restored cabin in Flora Park. Club members had removed the siding and plaster from the old farmhouse that had been built over the log cabin. After the building was hauled into town and placed in the park, they remodeled the cabin, added needed logs, repaired the roof, and added mortar. Decorated for the holidays as it might have been more than a hundred years before, the cabin provided a most appropriate setting as the teenagers made ornaments, exchanged gifts, and sang carols.[23]

The summer program for 1989 was less successful than those of previous years. Two scheduled activities were canceled due to lack of response. One was an archaeological project at Kampsville, Illinois, similar to the 1980 workshop. Instruction was to be provided at an actual excavation with attention given to special skill activities, such as toolmaking and ceramics. The other, in Indianapolis, was a publications workshop, designed to give juniors a chance to work with editors, photographers, and printers on an IJHS publication.[24] No canoe trip was planned. Instead, the summer activities were the Muscatatuck workshop and the two weeks of Little Hoosier camp. Both of these, however, were well attended and successful.

By the fall of 1989, the IJHS entered the third stage of development as outlined by Tom Krasean. This third stage was marked by increasing turmoil as a small group of sponsors, including Glen Dillman, Ron Morris, and Joyce Chambers, and several IJHS alumni became more critical of the Bureau's priorities. The executive committee of the Indiana Historical Society asked IJHS founder and Society trustee Richard S. Simons to chair an Ad Hoc Committee on Junior Historical Societies, "after a number of dedicated teachers and students, fearing adverse effects on their program[s] as the result of administrative changes by the Indiana Historical Bureau . . . voiced concern to the Society." Krasean and Dillman were members of the committee.[25]

Meanwhile Kevin Stonerock resigned on 1 September 1989 for personal reasons. "The decision to do so, made after careful consideration, was a difficult one," he told IJHS members. An article recapping Stonerock's many contributions to the IJHS indicated that he intended to take "his three living history personalities 'on the road' professionally as an independent artist."[26]

Bennett named Catherine Swanson to succeed Stonerock on 4 October 1989. A published poet and essayist, the Pennsylvania native was a graduate of both Ball State University and Indiana University and had a master's degree in folklore. In an upbeat introductory message to members Swanson noted the "solid foundation of enthusiastic, hard-working people in our organization" and the "legacy of the committed leadership of past directors." She concluded with the hope that the IJHS could "move forward in partnership to find new and better ways of collaborating to make history fun!"[27]

Despite her optimism, Swanson's appointment garnered criticism from long-standing IJHS supporters because of her lack of ties to the juniors. "Thus, the continuity that had been the driving force of the organization was broken," said Krasean.[28] "Whether the new IJHS director has or can develop the same passion for the IJHS program, exhibited by the former leadership, remains to be seen. No doubt some changes will be made. This very fact has upset a number of teachers and sponsors, and that is why they have turned to the Indiana Historical Society."[29]

The Ad Hoc Committee met four times: as an individual unit; with Bennett; with Stonerock; and with fourteen teachers from throughout the state. In its report dated 18 May 1990 the committee advocated "the strongest active support from the Society" and outlined four possible courses of action:

1. Assume complete control of the junior movement, either through the present organization or by establishing a new one.

Kevin Stonerock presents awards.
Indiana Historical Bureau

(Top, left) Kevin Stonerock and Glen Dillman. *Indiana Historical Bureau*
(Top, right) Kevin Stonerock and Jay Wilson in Civil War attire.
Indiana Historical Bureau

(Bottom) White River canoe trip, 1988. *Indiana Historical Bureau*

(Top) Carroll County log cabin. *Glen Dillman*

(Bottom, left) Ron Morris. *Courtesy of Ron Morris*
(Bottom, right) Catherine Swanson. *Indiana Historical Bureau*

(Top) Alice Wilson and campers at Columbus Youth Camp. *Indiana Historical Bureau*

(Bottom) Campers making cornhusk dolls. *Indiana Historical Bureau*

2. Increase present financial and/or organizational backing.
3. Maintain the status quo.
4. Withdraw all support.[30]

The committee believed that "a moderately aggressive course, as embodied in Option 2, would serve the best interests of everyone." To fulfill the Society's obligation to all Hoosiers who are interested in history, the Ad Hoc Committee made the following recommendations to the Society's executive committee and board of trustees:

1. Continue funding at not less than the present level.
2. Place the Junior Society under control of a board which shall consist of representatives of the Bureau, Society, and members, sponsors, and alumni of the Junior Society.
3. Forge closer ties between the Society and the Junior Society.
4. Maintain or increase summer activities.[31]

Five more supplemental recommendations defined additional projects the Ad Hoc Committee believed the Society should undertake to support the juniors.

After the Ad Hoc Committee made its report, Bennett established a Sponsor Advisory Board and named Krasean to it, a move the Society regarded as positive, because it created a "channel for dialogue" and allowed the Society to monitor IJHS activities more closely and tightened accountability for the Society's financial support.[32]

In August 1990 the Society's executive committee went on record as "favoring the present level of funding for the state's fiscal year ending 30 June 1991."[33] The executive committee approved a number of the ad hoc group's recommendations to increase the ties between the IJHS and the Society, including reestablishing a standing Junior Societies committee and incorporating the juniors into many existing activities, but it stopped short of endorsing any measures that would make the Society wholly responsible for the administration of the juniors program.

By April 1991, however, the Society's executive committee formally recommended that the juniors committee and the Society staff "consider the financial, administrative, and housing ramifications of the Indiana Historical Society undertaking the IJHS program."[34] By that time most parties regarded the Society's assumption of administrative oversight of the juniors as a welcome and sensible solution. The Bureau was expected to support the transition and continue to produce publications for the IJHS.

For Bennett and her colleagues at the Bureau, management of the IJHS, which benefited a relatively small number of Indiana schoolchildren, had become cumbersome, particularly in light of rigid state procurement regulations and salary structures. Bennett told Harstad that "the proposed division of responsibility for the program would help us both to carry out best the program and our missions."[35]

Administration of the IJHS would give the Society responsibility for an organization it had sustained financially since 1976. More important, as the Ad Hoc Committee had realized a year earlier, the IJHS was "the seed bed from which the Society may most easily perpetuate itself." The chance to work directly with students and sponsors in one of the leading junior movements in the nation was too promising to pass up. The Ad Hoc Committee had emphasized that "such a rare opportunity to strengthen itself may not again be presented to the Society in the near future."[36]

While adults deliberated over the future management of the IJHS, students participated in the usual array of IJHS activities, workshops, and the annual convention under Swanson's leadership through 1990 and into 1991. In 1990 Virginia Terpening served as director of what were to be the final sessions of IJHS summer camp offered at Muscatatuck.

In March 1991 the Bureau announced that Little Hoosier Summer Camp would be operated for two one-week sessions at the Columbus, Indiana, Youth Camp rather than the Jennings County site that had housed the program since 1972. "The new camp will house campers in cabins and offer a lake for waterfront activities," stated the announcement, which also outlined scheduling and class changes.[37]

Newly named Camp Director Tony Littell, a fourth-grade teacher at Mt. Healthy Elementary School in Columbus and a Little Hoosier sponsor for ten years, explained the program and changes in a letter to parents, stating that the maximum enrollment was 110 children per session and the fee would be fifty-five dollars. "Clearly it costs more than this amount to provide a week's camp experience. The remaining camp costs are subsidized by the Indiana Historical Society," said Littell.[38]

By the time the Little Hoosiers gathered at the Columbus Youth Camp in July 1991 to participate in Native American Village Life or French Settlement Life, responsibility for administering the IJHS had formally passed from the Indiana Historical Bureau to the Indiana Historical Society. While campers were making leather pouches and cornhusk dolls, leaping into their new lake, and folk dancing, Bureau and Society leaders were carrying out the logistical details of the transition, and the Society was searching for a new director.

Catherine Swanson resigned from the Bureau in April 1991 to pursue her interests in folklore and oral history research. Her graceful message to IJHS members included a reminder familiar to historians of any age: "It's the certainty of change which is unchanging! Being able to deal with change is a strength, one which this organization has demonstrated many times in its fifty-year history."[39]

By November 1991 Nancy Wolfe, the new director of the Indiana Junior Historical Society, was exhorting her juniors to look ahead. "As your new director I hope to see the IJHS grow and expand its programming," she wrote in her introductory message.[40] Sponsors and juniors ventured into the last decade of the twentieth century with well-founded confidence in the strength of their organization.

CHAPTER 7

Sixty Years Strong

Befitting an organization rooted in the past and focused on the future, the Indiana Junior Historical Society ended 1991, its first year under new leadership, by marking an important military milestone and drumming up interest in activities for the following year.

To remember the fiftieth anniversary of Pearl Harbor, new director Nancy Wolfe included in the December 1991 newsletter an excerpt of a letter written by Hoosier Jearl Driscoll.

> I'll never forget Christmas Eve of 1944. I was in Europe stationed at a heavy equipment depot attached to the 9th Army. . . . It was bitterly cold and very foggy. I ran everywhere because the only coat I had was my combat jacket.

With her educator's instincts and long-standing interest in the American Civil War, Wolfe also ran a portion of the Christmas Eve entry from the Civil War diary of Alva C. Griest of Crawfordsville.

> In what novel manner I am celebrating it here. I am wet, muddy, and in no amicable humor at the root of a giant oak, solitary and alone.[1]

It is not hard to imagine Wolfe wanting to wrap some of her handmade quilts around these shivering soldiers to soothe and encourage them. The Fort Wayne native and former Little Hoosier sponsor had a decade of teaching experience before she became the education coordinator for the Indiana State Museum in Indianapolis in 1990, and less than two years later, the successor to Catherine Swanson. A nurturer at heart, more likely to greet a visitor with a hug than a handshake, Wolfe used her gentle manners and genuine enthusiasm to redirect the juniors organization and meet the expectations and requirements of its sponsoring society.

Wolfe knew there were bridges to mend and serious issues to address, and in the first few weeks she felt overwhelmed. "There was no one here to train me, but I had a stack of records on my desk from the Bureau and a workshop to attend a week after I arrived," she said. "I remember sitting at the workshop thinking, 'I'm Bob Kirby now. Maybe I should growl,'" referring to the juniors' former director.[2]

"I relied a lot on my experience as an IJr.HS sponsor. Many people wanted us to keep things the way they were when Mr. Kirby and Mr. Stonerock led the organization. I can't ever be them, and besides, the IJr.HS is not the same," said Wolfe. "We were much stronger and able to do more now that we were under the Indiana Historical Society umbrella. I also felt strongly that even though 'history is fun,' it needed to be more than just fun. If the IJr.HS was to remain a unique organization we had to be not only fun but also giving back to the Society and our communities and strengthening our students' historical and educational perspectives."[3]

Armed with these convictions, Wolfe wasted no time. The December 1991 newsletter also included pleas for a chapter to host the Junior-Senior Convention the following April, entries for the juniors' T-shirt design contest, and chapter news items for the monthly newsletter.

Wolfe quickly realized that she could not accomplish her goals—or anyone else's—without some help. That help arrived in early 1992 in the form of longtime Indiana Historical Society staff member Patricia Gillogly, who worked for both the juniors and Thomas K. Krasean in community relations for about a year before she became the full-time administrative associate for the IJr.HS.

"She was looking for a place to grow, and she's really done that because I keep giving her more and more to do," said Wolfe with a grateful laugh. Gillogly's administrative skill and easy rapport with the students have kept countless meetings and workshops productive and on schedule.

Two of Wolfe and Gillogly's initial and most important tasks were to revise the juniors' constitution and to update and publish a new handbook for sponsors. Wolfe enlisted the help of the rejuvenated IJr.HS Advisory Board for the constitution project, asking selected sponsors (from all divisions), staff members, IHS Board of Trustee representatives, and state officers to meet in Indianapolis in August 1992 to present and discuss proposed revisions.[4] "The previous version was out of date, particularly with the new management structure," said Wolfe. "Since we were no longer part of a state agency, we could not use the seal, and there was a real need for more definitions and consistency." The revised constitution was ratified by members via mail ballot in November 1992.[5]

Also in late 1992 the juniors, as part of a reorganization of the Indiana Historical Society, moved from the administrative division to the newly created education division directed by Robert M. Taylor, Jr., who joined the IJr.HS's advisory board. The education division was created "to coordinate the various areas of the society dealing with education, research projects, grants, exhibits, the talking books program, and local historical groups."[6]

Gillogly handled many aspects of producing the sponsors' handbook, which covered everything from bylaws and state officer qualifications to convention award descriptions. A model of clarity, the manual was revised in 1996. "The sponsors loved it," admitted Wolfe. "They had been

(Top) Nancy Wolfe with students. *IJr.HS (IHS)*

(Bottom, left) Pat Gillogly. *IHS*
(Bottom, right) Robert M. Taylor, Jr. *IHS*

Candy Taff Carr. *IHS*

Conventions, 1990s. *IJr.HS (IHS)*

working from several different versions and really needed something more helpful. Sponsors themselves contributed step-by-step instructions in some sections, including Candace Taff Carr of the W. D. Richards Little Hoosiers in Columbus who wrote "Making a Slide Program or Filmstrip of Your Community's History," and Glen Dillman, sponsor of the Sycamore Club in Carroll County, who produced "Setting Up a Pioneer Festival" and "Guidelines for Building an Exhibit."[7] Sponsor guidelines had appeared in various versions of previous handbooks.

By 1993 leaders of the IJr.HS decided to combine the annual conventions of the Little Hoosier and junior-senior divisions and add new contests, competitions, and rules for participating. Many of the previous awards and activities were preserved, but for the first time guidelines and standards were streamlined, defined, and made available to all IJr.HS members and their sponsors.

"Not only were trophies and plaques given, but cash awards were added," said Wolfe. "We felt that some of the convention budget would be best spent by giving it back to chapters for continuation of their outstanding programs at their schools and [in their] local communities. We also added a sponsor award to recognize their contributions to the IJr.HS."[8]

North Central High School and John Strange Elementary School in Indianapolis welcomed a total of 850 students and sponsors to the 14–15 May 1993 gathering.[9] The combined format was received with enthusiasm. "Each member and chapter participating in the 1992–93 Annual Convention contributed to the great success of a combined convention," recounted an article in a subsequent newsletter. "The caliber of entries in all contests was excellent."[10] Wolfe saw additional advantages. "The combined convention offered elementary students an opportunity to see older students in leadership roles, and in turn the junior-senior members got to see the really inspirational work the younger students put forth," she said.[11]

Works created for the 1996 convention at Randolph Southern Junior-Senior High School in Lynn, attended by some six hundred individuals, were used to construct an Indiana Historical Society exhibition titled "A Junior Sampler," which was displayed in the Society's lobby for several months. Among the remarkable chapters recognized at that convention was the Conner Prairie Junior Historical Society, a group of home-schooled children sponsored by parents. "Members of that chapter raised money to travel to historic sites in and around Philadelphia," reported Wolfe in the Society's newsletter. She later noted that groups sponsored by parents, libraries, and entities other than schools made up a small but strong segment of the junior society's membership.[12]

The joint structure continued successfully through 1997, when 450 participants drove to Edison Junior-Senior High School in Lake Station for the annual gathering on 2–3 May, hosted jointly by the Carl Polk Little Hoosiers, Edison Historians, and Hobart Historians. "The drop in attendance was due to the location," observed Wolfe. The convention had never been held that far north, so some chapters in the southern half of the state were unable to attend. Many students who participated, however, experienced the Dunes region for the first time.[13] Activities included presentations on Civil War medicine, regional history, pioneer toys and games, and LTV Steel. Wolfe noted that the host chapters had secured one thousand dollars in private donations for programs and food.[14]

Changing interests, creative ideas, and liability concerns prompted IJr.HS leaders to modify and expand summer program options throughout the 1990s. "We compete with Little League, sports camps, church camps, family vacations, 4-H, Girl Scout and Boy Scout camps, summer school, year-round schools, and other local day camps," said Wolfe.[15]

Little Hoosier Camp continued at the Columbus Youth Camp, but attendance dropped from 200 in three sessions in 1993 to about 130 in two sessions in 1997.[16] Wolfe announced in 1994 that she was working with the American Camping Association (ACA) to make changes and long-term improvements in the camp program. In particular she was looking for guidelines on issues of camp liability. She added a registered nurse and an assistant director to the staff and upgraded counselor training to help director Fred Williams strengthen the Little Hoosiers camp program. ACA assistance "has been a great help," said Wolfe in 1997.[17]

Wolfe also began looking at other camp facilities in Indiana, anticipating that the Columbus Youth Camp site owners might not be able to accommodate the juniors in future summers. By late 1997 she announced that the 1998 summer camp would take place at Walnut Hills Retreat near Trevlac in Brown County. Her long-term goal was to employ a new IJr.HS staff member directly responsible for the summer camp program.

According to Wolfe, "the new site will be smaller and we will return to three weeks of camp. The theme will be new also. Students get a lot of pioneer and Indian stuff at school, at festivals, and within their own chapters. They need to do something new, so the first new camp theme will deal with architecture. We will offer staff orientation in March for the first time."[18]

The decision to focus on architecture in the summer programs was not without precedent for the junior society. Although activities in the late 1990s promised to be innovative and creative, the juniors would be pursuing an interest that had captivated their predecessors three decades earlier. Bob Montgomery, the man who started the architectural surveys in the late 1960s, would probably have applauded Nancy Wolfe's decisions in the late 1990s.

Bus trips, cemetery searches, research projects, and leadership workshops continued to attract students in the upper grades and their sponsors in the summer months and on weekends during the academic year. When the older students were not helping with Little Hoosier camp in the summer, they could take two-day excursions into various regions of Indiana or take on comprehensive projects farther afield.

In December 1992 the IJr.HS offered students in the junior-senior division the opportunity to participate in a major undertaking involving research on an Indiana soldier, regiment, or ancestor who had engaged in the Battle of Shiloh in southwestern Tennessee from 6–7 April 1862. Participants were expected to submit a one-page essay of

Papermaking at Walnut Hills camp. *IJr.HS (IHS)*

(Top) Grant Goshorn at Shiloh. *IJr.HS (IHS)*

(Bottom) Shiloh. *IJr.HS (IHS)*

intent and goals by 15 February 1993, a written paper of no less than fifteen hundred words about their findings by 31 May, and an oral project presentation to be delivered at a one-day symposium. A summer field trip to Shiloh National Military Park in the summer of 1993 was the incentive offered by the IJr.HS to students completing all requirements.[19]

Thirteen junior-senior members made commitments to the Shiloh project, and that summer they hiked fourteen miles in the park, answering questions about the battle as they traveled. They also enjoyed a riverboat cruise and had a progressive dinner in some of the oldest and largest antebellum mansions outside Nashville. "The students' impressive research efforts brought accolades from Tennesseans who hosted many of the week's activities," Wolfe proudly stated.[20]

One of the Shiloh project participants was Grant Goshorn, then a member of the Tipton History Hunters. Several years later, when he was a senior at Columbus East High School and president of the IJr.HS, Goshorn recalled his solitary visit to an empty field at Shiloh as the most inspirational moment of his life.

The empty field was where William H. Hook, a sergeant from my county, had fought his first battle. I had become acquainted with Hook by looking through obituaries, war records, and old newspapers. While I had read accounts of the battle written by other men in his regiment, I could not picture what he saw until I spent time at Shiloh. Only then could I start to feel Hook's fear, pain, and courage. Only then did history become real.[21]

Bus tours became increasingly popular ways to involve students in the junior-senior division and expose sponsors to educational opportunities and programs around the state. A two-day tour in August 1995 took seventeen students on a history of flight, traveling to the United States Air Force Museum in Dayton, Ohio, and the Challenger Learning Center of Brownsburg, Indiana. Twice as many students participated in the 1996 summer bus tour of the Ohio River region, which included stops at the Falls of the Ohio State Park, the *Belle of Louisville* steamboat, the Marengo Cave, and a buffalo farm in Needmore. The 1997 tour, dubbed History Cruiser II, attracted twenty-six students for stops in northwestern Indiana at LTV Steel, the Indiana Dunes State Park, the Old Lighthouse at Michigan City, and Indiana's International Port at Portage.

A six-day trip slated for 1998 took the juniors even farther afield. Students explored the Underground Railroad, traveling from New Albany into Canada. They also produced a video journal of the trip.

In a concerted effort to enhance sponsor training, provide curriculum support materials for teachers, and, of course, to appeal to new sponsors, the IJr.HS staff organized a number of trips and daylong seminars strictly for educators and alumni. Twenty-two sponsors and IJr.HS alumni traveled to western Indiana in 1996 to visit Billie Creek Village, the Ernie Pyle State Historic Site, Turkey Run State Park, and other Parke County sites.[22]

Wolfe and Gillogly often brought together educational organizations from around the state to describe IJr.HS programs to the adults in a single setting. In August 1994, for

In the summer of 1995 on a two-day tour detailing the history of flight, students explored the United States Air Force Museum, Dayton, Ohio, and the Challenger Learning Center, Brownsburg, Indiana. *IJr.HS (IHS)*

Alan Goldstein (with the Department of Natural Resources) talks with participants of the 1997 IJr.HS/GENI Institute at the Falls of the Ohio. *IJr.HS (IHS)*

example, sponsors gathered at the Indiana State Library for presentations by the Geography Educators Network of Indiana (GENI), the Indiana Humanities Council, the Indiana Council for the Social Studies, the Indiana Arts Commission, and Young Audiences of Indiana. Afternoon field trip opportunities included the Madame C. J. Walker Theatre, the Indiana Medical History Museum, and the Morris-Butler House.[23]

In August 1996 twenty teachers had a chance to earn three hours of graduate credit in education by participating in a weeklong institute on the history and geography of the National Lakeshore and Calumet Region of Indiana.[24] IJr.HS staff members worked with the Geography Educators Network of Indiana to develop and conduct the first-of-its-kind institute. Sites for field experiences included the Pinhook Bog, Beverly Shores, the Michigan City Public Library, and the Bailly Homestead–Chellburg Farm. Representatives from Historic Landmarks Foundation of Indiana, Calumet Regional Archives, Michigan City Public Library, and the Indiana Dunes National Lakeshore participated in these activities.

The IJr.HS and GENI turned south to another body of water for a second institute for teachers in July 1997, this one titled "Exploring and Teaching . . . Indiana's Ohio River Valley." Thirty-five teachers participated, half of whom were expected to earn graduate credit from Indiana University Southeast.[25]

In addition to inviting other state organizations to work with IJr.HS sponsors, Wolfe and Gillogly frequently made presentations to outside groups as part of an overall outreach effort that includes consultation with state curriculum policy makers. They continued the IJr.HS's tradition of providing programs to chapters and groups interested in forming chapters throughout the state. In 1995 the IJr.HS hired Foster Brown as a field representative. In 1996 he made twenty-six visits and shared history with nearly eighteen hundred students and was later succeeded by juniors veteran Kevin Stonerock.[26]

Gillogly edits the juniors' newsletter, *IJr.HS Notes,* issued eight times a year, to stay in touch with chapters and highlight outstanding members and activities. The newsletter sports an attractive logo designed by Deb Larimore of Muncie. Students selected the new symbol from three proposed designs at the 1992 convention.[27]

In 1997 Wolfe reported that she was exploring the concept of corporate sponsorship with Advisory Board chairman Mary Jane Meeker and Society trustee Larry Pitts. Under consideration was the acquisition of an IJr.HS van to promote (and transport) the juniors around the state.[28]

The outreach efforts were essential to keep new members and sponsors coming in to the IJr.HS as students graduated and sponsors retired or moved on to other obligations. Throughout the 1990s the number of chapters ranged from 124 to 132, and the total number of members fluctuated mildly between a 1994 high of 4,900 and a more typical figure of 4,300 in 1997.

"There are growth issues, and of course I would like to see more members," acknowledged Wolfe. "Growth issues stem from teacher retirements, school mergers and closings, teacher classroom and building changes, and changes

Pat Gillogly edits the newly formatted *IJr.HS Notes.*
IJr.HS (IHS)

Jessica Beeson in 1990s garb (above) and dressed in vintage clothing with three generations of her family. *IJr.HS (IHS)*

New IHS headquarters. *IHS*

in school populations. But I am not unhappy with our numbers. Some states don't even have groups like this any more, and we are still going strong."[29]

And strong the juniors are, observing their sixtieth anniversary in 1998. Perhaps the unsung heroes of the Indiana Junior Historical Society for six decades have been the parents who have gathered supplies, proofread reports, display boards, and speeches, and made long treks around Indiana so their children could attend conventions, camps, and workshops. Although they often devoted the same hours the students and teachers put in, they were usually in the background and on the sidelines when the cheering began. And for most of them, that was more than enough.

Up in the bleachers of the gymnasium at Randolph County Junior-Senior High School in Lynn, Paula Beeson sat on a Saturday afternoon in May 1996, proudly watching her daughter Jessica, then in sixth grade, receive recognition as the junior director of the north division for the next two years. Beeson had no complaints about leaving her Kokomo home at 6:00 A.M. Jessica's interest in history was a family trait—her grandmother and Paula's mother, Joann Weisner, collected vintage clothing.

As a middle schooler, Jessica had moved out of the Little Hoosier division and was participating in the IJr.HS as an individual member. "She wants to stay active and run for office and rejuvenate the high school chapter," said her mother. "Jessica kept asking questions about staying involved. She's done it on her own and has continued while others have dropped out."[30]

Jessica Beeson was elected secretary of the IJr.HS in 1997. Her commendable persistence was a reflection of her mother's support and personal enthusiasm. Four generations of Beeson women attended the 1997 Leadership Workshop for officers in the junior-senior division, where Jessica and her mother modeled some of Mrs. Weisner's best finds in a vintage fashion show titled "I Can't Believe You Wore That!" Even Jessica's great-grandmother was on hand for the display.

That sort of family involvement is something Jessica Beeson may appreciate fully only when she swats at a blaring alarm clock at 5:00 A.M. sometime in the next century to take her own offspring and their treasures on field trips, workshops, and visits to historical sites.

When the Indiana Junior Historical Society celebrated its sixtieth anniversary in 1998, members spent time helping Wolfe and Gillogly box up records and select artifacts and awards to display in the IJr.HS's offices in the Indiana Historical Society's new building at the corner of Ohio and West Streets, which opened in July 1999.

The new offices are lovely, record keeping is easier, and Wolfe and Gillogly enjoy having more than twenty-four inches between their desks in a converted closet, but the juniors have never depended on fancy trappings for success. The state has benefited from projects designed by the juniors for the new exhibit areas, and citizens have had many opportunities to watch juniors perform in the Society's new classrooms and public spaces.

But out in the field, down at camp, and in classrooms across Indiana, the juniors need to flourish as well away from the central headquarters. Inspiring curiosity about

Club activities. *IJr.HS (IHS)*

this state has become an honored tradition for a small but tenacious group of citizens that began with Richard S. Simons and continued with Mike Westfall and Marcy McDowell and Jon Turpin and Debbie Fausset and Kevin Stonerock and Allison Moore and David Roberts and Jessica Beeson and Abby Thom and Grant Goshorn, and the list goes on and on.

Former juniors have revived the IJr.HS Alumni Association, which has provided camp photos and operated camp snack sales since 1993. The group meets twice a year and uses the funds it raises to send sponsors to workshops and allocate programming grants and scholarships to local chapters.[31]

The Indiana Junior Historical Society, a group that operated rather well out of Bob Montgomery's back pocket for ten years, just might find a way to maintain satellite chapters on a space station sometime in the next century. With an alumni group gaining in numbers and influence, and eager Little Hoosiers clamoring for more activities, this intergenerational association of time travelers can keep up its tradition of "looking at the past through the eyes of the future."

Notes

Editor's Note: The junior society used the IJHS acronym from 1938 until 1991, when the organization adopted the IJr.HS abbreviation. This history will follow the same pattern.

Chapter 1

1. Mike Bonne, "Goddard School," *Indiana History Bulletin* 51 (Nov. 1974): 149–50.

2. Glen Dillman, telephone interview with Kendal Gladish, 3 June 1996.

3. Nancy Wolfe, "IJr.HS Sponsor Unites Community through History," *The Bridge* 1, no. 5 (Sept.–Oct. 1995).

4. Bill Wepler, telephone interview with Kendal Gladish, 24 June 1996.

5. Nancy Wolfe, "Juniors Clean Current Cemetery," *The Bridge* 1, no. 5 (Sept.–Oct. 1995).

6. Kevin Stonerock, "From the Director," *Newsletter, Indiana Junior Historical Society,* Jr./Sr. Div. (Nov. 1988): 1.

7. Steve Catron, Abby McConnell, Dana Marcellino, and Christopher Moore, interviews with Kendal Gladish, Lynn, Ind., 11 May 1996.

8. *IJr.HS Notes* 5, no. 1 (Sept. 1996).

9. Dillman, telephone interview.

10. Nancy Wolfe, telephone interviews with Kendal Gladish, 16 May, 20 June 1996.

11. Marjorie Snodgrass, telephone interview with Kendal Gladish, 20 Sept. 1996.

12. Fred Williams, interview with Kendal Gladish, Lynn, Ind., 11 May 1996.

13. Wolfe, telephone interviews.

14. Ron Woodward, telephone interview with Kendal Gladish, 19 June 1996.

15. Tammy Artis, interview with Kendal Gladish, Lynn, Ind., 11 May 1996.

16. David Roberts, "President's Message," *IJr.HS Notes* 1, no. 8 (1 Apr. 1993).

17. Ibid., telephone interview with Kendal Gladish, 3 June 1996.

18. Mike Westfall, interview with Kendal Gladish, Indianapolis, 27 June 1996.

19. Mary Fortney, telephone interviews with Kendal Gladish, 23 May, 11 July 1996.

20. Woodward, telephone interview.

21. "The Forty-Sixth Annual Session of the Indiana State Teachers Association, 26, 27, 28, and 29 December" (Indianapolis, 1899), in *Indiana State Teachers Association Programs, 1895–1900.*

22. Department of Public Instruction, State of Indiana, *State Manual and Uniform Course of Study for the Elementary and High Schools of Indiana* (Indianapolis: Wm. P. Burford, 1899), appendix IV, p. 160.

23. Ibid., 161.

24. Harlow Lindley, ed., *The Indiana Centennial, 1916: A Record of the Celebration of the One Hundredth Anniversary of Indiana's Admission to Statehood,* vol. 5 of *Indiana Historical Collections* (Indianapolis: Indiana Historical Commission, 1919), 33.

25. Ibid., 33.

26. Ibid., 33–34.

27. Ibid., 26.

28. Herbert Briggs, "The Present Status of Indiana History in the Schools," *Indiana History Bulletin,* Extra Number (Feb. 1925): 57.

29. Ibid., 58.

30. Ibid., 59.

31. Oscar H. Williams, letter to John W. Oliver, 10 Apr. 1922, file: A4399, box 1, Junior Historical Societies 1922 folder, Indiana Historical Bureau, IJHS Records, Indiana State Archives, Commission on Public Records, Indianapolis.

32. John W. Oliver and Oscar H. Williams, letter to Roy B. Julian, 27 Mar. 1922, ibid.

33. Oscar H. Williams, "Junior Historical Societies," *Indiana History Bulletin,* Extra Number (Feb. 1925): 53.

34. Ibid., 54–55.

35. Lana Ruegamer, *A History of the Indiana Historical Society, 1830–1980* (Indianapolis: Indiana Historical Society, 1980), 167.

36. Christopher Coleman, "Junior Historians," *Indiana History Bulletin* 18 (Feb. 1941): 137.

37. Ruegamer, *History of the Indiana Historical Society,* 167–68; *Indiana History Bulletin* 16 (May 1939): 195.

38. "History Club Activities," *Indiana History Bulletin* 16 (May 1939): 194.

39. "Teacher-Student History Convention at Marion," *Indiana History Bulletin* 15 (Apr. 1938): 206–7.

40. Indiana Department of Public Instruction, *Annual Reports,* 1936–42, p. 449.

41. *Indiana History Bulletin* 15 (Apr. 1938): 206.

42. "Program for the Indiana Teacher-Student History Convention, April 9, 1938, Marion, Indiana," Indiana Historical Bureau, IJHS Records, Indiana State Archives, Commission on Public Records.

43. Christopher Coleman, "Reports of Committees: Executive Committee," *Indiana History Bulletin* 16 (Feb. 1939): 42.

44. John Overman, "Junior Historical Societies and History Clubs," ibid., 99.

45. Quoted in William H. McGrew, "Historic Spots Lack Markers," *Marion Sunday Chronicle Tribune,* 24 July 1955.

46. Horace Bailey Carroll, "The Junior Historian Movement in Public Schools," *Texas Historian* 49, no. 5 (May 1989): 17.

47. Quoted in Dorman H. Winfrey, "The Junior Historians: The Early Years," ibid., 7.

48. "The Indiana History Conference," *Indiana History Bulletin* 15 (Dec. 1938): 362.

49. *Indiana History Bulletin* 16 (May 1939): 193.

50. "Junior Historical Organizations," *Indiana History Bulletin* 17 (May 1940): 232.

51. Indiana Junior Historical Society Constitution (Apr. 1940), Article III, section E, printed in *Indiana History Bulletin* 18 (Jan. 1941): 7–11.

52. *Bulletin: Indiana Junior Historical Society* (Nov. 1941–42), file: A4399, box 1, Junior Historical Society 1939–45 folder, Indiana Historical Bureau, IJHS Records, Indiana State Archives, Commission on Public Records.

53. "Committees of the Indiana Historical Society," *Indiana History Bulletin* 16 (Apr. 1939): 173.

54. *Warren Central Bulletin of Indiana History* (Dec. 1941).

55. "Junior Historical Societies," *Indiana History Bulletin* 18 (May 1941): 232.

56. Ibid. (Dec. 1941): 417–18.

57. "Indiana Junior Historical Society Annual Meeting, April 19," *Indiana History Bulletin* (Apr. 1941): 207.

58. "Program for the Fourth Annual Convention, Arsenal Technical Schools, Indianapolis, April 19, 1941," Indiana Historical Bureau, IJHS Records, Indiana State Archives, Commission on Public Records.

59. *Indiana History Bulletin* 18 (Feb. 1941): 138; *Bulletin: Indiana Junior Historical Society* (Oct. 1941–42); (Nov. 1941–42); *The Junior Historian* (Jan. 1941–42).

60. *The Junior Historian* (Jan. 1941–42).

61. *Bulletin: Indiana Junior Historical Society* (Oct. 1941–42), file: A4399, box 1, Junior Historical Society folder, Indiana Historical Bureau, IJHS Records, Indiana State Archives, Commission on Public Records.

Chapter 2

1. "Program for the Fifth Annual Convention, Aurora, Indiana, March 28, 1942," Indiana Historical Bureau, IJHS Records, Indiana State Archives, Commission on Public Records, Indianapolis.

2. *Indiana History Bulletin* 19 (Apr. 1942): 140.

3. *Bulletin: Indiana Junior Historical Society* (Apr. 1942).

4. *Indiana History Bulletin* 19 (Mar. 1942): 101.

5. "Junior Historical Society," *Indiana History Bulletin* 22 (Nov. 1945): 326.

6. *Arsenal Cannon* (yearbook), Arsenal Technical Schools, 1941–42.

7. *Indiana History Bulletin* 21 (Jan. 1944): 54.

8. Ibid. 20 (May 1943): 223–24.

9. Ibid. 21 (May 1944): 210; 22 (Nov. 1945): 326.

10. *Warren Central Bulletin of Indiana History* (Apr.–May 1945).

11. *Indiana History Bulletin* 22 (June 1945): 168.

12. Ibid. 23 (Jan. 1946): 99–100.

13. Letter from Committee, addressed to "Dear Teacher," 11 Nov. 1945.

14. *Indiana History Bulletin* 25 (Feb. 1948): 51.

15. Howard Peckham, letter to Richard Simons, 17 Apr. 1947, file: A4399, box 1, Indiana Junior Historical Society 1948–50 folder, Indiana Historical Bureau, IJHS Records, Indiana State Archives, Commission on Public Records.

16. Peckham, letter to Richard Simons and Alberta Cannon, 19 May 1947, ibid.

17. *Indiana History Bulletin* 25 (Feb. 1948): 50–51.

18. State Department of Public Instruction, questionnaire, Jan. 1949, correspondence file, 1949–51, Indiana Historical Bureau, IJHS Records, Indiana State Archives, Commission on Public Records.

19. Indiana Historical Bureau, *Biennial Report, 1948–50* (Indianapolis, 1950), 12.

20. *Indiana History Bulletin* 27 (Jan. 1950): 31–32.

21. Ibid., 33.

22. Ibid. 26 (May 1949): 92; 27 (Jan. 1950): 33.

23. *Hoosier Historian* 1, no. 2 (Oct. 1949).

24. *Indiana History Bulletin* 26 (May 1949): 92.

25. *Hoosier Historian* 1, no. 2 (Oct. 1949).

26. *Biennial Report, 1948–50,* p. 12.

27. "Indiana State School Facilities Survey, RSA-6 Report to the United States Office of Education, November 30, 1951," report, Indiana Division, Indiana State Library, Indianapolis.

28. *Hoosier Historian* 1, no. 8 (May 1950).

29. Ibid.

30. Quoted in Richard Simons, "History on Location," *Indianapolis Star Sunday Magazine,* 23 Apr. 1950.

31. Peckham, letter to Wilbur H. Young, 15 Jan. 1951, correspondence file, 1949–51, Indiana Historical Bureau, IJHS Records, Indiana State Archives, Commission on Public Records.

32. Peckham, letter to Glenn Neeves, 14 Feb. 1951, file: A4400, box 2, ibid.

33. *Indiana History Bulletin* 28 (Sept. 1951): 145.

34. Richard Haupt, letter to Hester Hale, 11 July 1989, author's (Hester Hale) files; *Hoosier Historian* 4, no. 1 (Oct. 1952).

35. Peckham, letter to Haupt, 15 Jan. 1952, file: A4400, box 2, Indiana Historical Bureau, IJHS Records, Indiana State Archives, Commission on Public Records.

36. Haupt, letter to Peckham, 6 Feb. 1952, ibid.

37. IJHS End of Year Report, 1952–53; Haupt, letter to Hale.

38. *Hoosier Historian* 4, no. 6 (May 1953).

39. Ibid. 1, no. 8 (May 1950).

40. Ibid. 2, no. 5 (May 1951).

41. Ibid. 3, no. 6 (May 1952).

42. Peckham, letter to Howard S. Wilcox, 12 Sept. 1951, file: A4400, box 2, Indiana Historical Bureau, IJHS Records, Indiana State Archives, Commission on Public Records.

43. *Hoosier Historian* 3, no. 6 (May 1952).

44. Ibid.

45. Ibid. 4, no. 6 (May 1953).

46. "Indiana Library and Historical Board Minutes," 19 Apr. 1954, Manuscripts, Indiana Division, Indiana State Library.

47. *Hoosier Historian* 6, no. 1 (Jan. 1955).

48. "Indiana Library and Historical Board Minutes," 21 July 1955, Manuscripts, Indiana Division, Indiana State Library.

49. Carl Zenor, interview with Hester Hale, 9 June 1989.

50. Zenor, letter to high school principals, 20 Feb. 1960, Indiana Historical Bureau, IJHS Records, Indiana State Archives, Commission on Public Records.

51. Indiana Junior Historical Society Year End Reports, 1958–59; 1959–60.

52. Lana Ruegamer, *A History of the Indiana Historical Society, 1830–1980* (Indianapolis: Indiana Historical Society, 1980), 72–73.

53. Ronald E. Young, "The History of School District Reorganization in the State of Indiana" (Ph.D. diss., Indiana University, 1968), 1, 65.

54. Ibid., 67, 88, 133.

55. Ibid., 162, 164.

Chapter 3

1. Carl Zenor, letter to Sister M. Evangela SS.C.M., 3 Oct. 1962, correspondence file, 1962–63, Indiana Historical Bureau, IJHS Records, Indiana State Archives, Commission on Public Records, Indianapolis.

2. *Hoosier Historian* 9, no. 4 (May 1958).

3. Robert Montgomery, "History for Young People," Technical Leaflet 44, in *History News* 22, no. 9 (Sept. 1967). Technical Leaflet 44 was revised and reprinted by the American Association for State and Local History (AASLH) in 1972.

4. Hubert Hawkins, letter to W. H. Skinner, 1 June 1965, personnel files, Indiana Historical Bureau, Indianapolis.

5. "The IJHS is Growing," *Indiana History Bulletin* 41 (Oct. 1964): 138.

6. Hawkins, letter to Skinner.

7. Howard Peckham, letter to Hazel Coyne, 26 Oct. 1949, file: A4399, box 1, Indiana Junior Historical Society 1948–50 folder, Indiana Historical Bureau, IJHS Records, Indiana State Archives, Commission on Public Records.

8. Joseph H. Wilhelm, "Research Brief," vol. 5, no. 1 (Apr. 1962). This is a collection of various statistics prepared for William E. Wilson, superintendent, Indiana Department of Public Instruction.

9. Ronald E. Young, "The History of School District Reorganization in the State of Indiana" (Ph.D. diss., Indiana University, 1968), 224.

10. Ibid., 318.

11. Montgomery, "History for Young People," Technical Leaflet 44 (1967).

12. Ibid., (1972).

13. *Indiana History Bulletin* 53 (Feb. 1976): 21.

14. Indiana Department of Public Instruction, *Expanding Experiences in the Elementary School*, bulletin no. 215 (1953), 86.

15. Ibid., bulletin no. 231 (1960), 68, 79.

16. "Interim Report of the State Committee for the Revision of the Social Studies" (23 Apr. 1963), pamphlet, Indiana State Library, Indianapolis.

17. Letter to William E. Wilson, 27 Apr. 1964 (unsigned carbon copy), Indiana Historical Bureau, IJHS Records, Indiana State Archives, Commission on Public Records.

18. *Indiana History Bulletin* 41 (Feb. 1964): 28.

19. Debbie Cramer, letter to Sen. J. J. Bailey, [before 5 Apr. 1967], Miscellaneous file, Indiana Historical Bureau, IJHS Records, Indiana State Archives, Commission on Public Records.

20. Edgar Smith, memo to all superintendents and principals, 12 Nov. 1965.

21. "Indiana State Board of Education Minutes," 9 July 1965.

22. Thomas S. Emison, letter to Sen. Robert Fair, 14 Feb. 1967, Indiana Historical Bureau, IJHS Records, Indiana State Archives, Commission on Public Records.

23. Cramer, letter to Bailey.

24. Bailey, letter to Cramer, 5 Apr. 1967, Indiana Historical Bureau, IJHS Records, Indiana State Archives, Commission on Public Records.

25. *Indiana History Bulletin* 44 (Jan. 1967): 4.

26. *A Handbook for History Club Officers and Sponsors* (Indianapolis, 1966), 22.

27. "Little Hoosier Historian Renewal Form," Activities Listing file, Indiana Historical Bureau, IJHS Records, Indiana State Archives, Commission on Public Records. This renewal, ca. 1968, shows Westwood as the first (Chapter #1) Little Hoosier Historian Club.

28. *ISTA News* 3, no. 9 (June 1967).

29. "Little Hoosier Historians Membership Now Available," *The Hoosier Schoolmaster* 6, no. 5 (Jan. 1967): 32.

30. *A Handbook for Little Hoosiers*, rev. ed. (1986), 6–7.

31. *Indiana History Bulletin* 37 (Mar. 1960): 23.

32. "Indiana Library and Historical Board Minutes," 21 July 1964, Manuscripts, Indiana Division, Indiana State Library; *Indiana History Bulletin* 42 (Aug. 1965): 119–20.

33. Hubert Hawkins, letter to Indiana Junior Historical Society

Chapters, 14 Oct. 1964, Special Bulletins file, Indiana Historical Bureau, IJHS Records, Indiana State Archives, Commission on Public Records.

34. Mildred Henricks, letter to Robert Montgomery, 15 Apr. 1965, correspondence file, 1964–65, ibid.

35. *Indiana History Bulletin* 6, extra no. 1 (Jan. 1929).

36. Anna Jane Miller, letter to IJHS Sesquicentennial Committee, 1 Sept. 1965, Sesquicentennial Committee file, Indiana Historical Bureau, IJHS Records, Indiana State Archives, Commission on Public Records; *IJHS Newsletter* (1 Jan. 1964).

37. *Indiana History Bulletin* 43 (Mar. 1966): 23.

38. *IJHS Newsletter* (3 Mar. 1965).

39. *Indiana Magazine of History* 62 (June 1966): 155–56.

40. *Indiana History Bulletin* 43 (Dec. 1966): 161.

41. *IJHS Newsletter* (16 Nov. 1966).

42. Ibid. (2 May 1966).

43. *Indiana History Bulletin* 44 (July 1967): 102.

44. *IJHS Newsletter* (8 Nov. 1967).

45. *Fort Wayne Journal-Gazette*, 17 Apr. 1966.

46. Mary I. Benedict, "Touring the Riley Trail: Arlington Knights Keep Date with History," *Indiana Teacher* 111 (May–June 1967): 280–81.

47. *IJHS Newsletter* (6 Oct. 1967).

48. Wilbur Peat, *Indiana Houses of the Nineteenth Century* (Indianapolis: Indiana Historical Society, 1962).

49. Mike Westfall, interview with Kendal Gladish, Indianapolis, 27 June 1996.

50. Ibid.

51. Al Hodge, interview with Hester Hale, 8 June 1989.

52. *Vernon: An Indiana Town, 1968* (Indianapolis: Indiana Junior Historical Society, 1968), 3. Other participants in the project were: Bill Hixon and David Hoggatt, Arlington High School; Kathy Cass and Theda Brannon, Northwest High School; Carolyn Martin, Howe High School; Kim Waters and Dyan Bricker, Oak Hill High School; Keah Hardisty, Kunieh Society; Barbara Perin, Rushville High School; Terry Anthony, Lewisville High School; and Deloris Gibson, Short High School.

53. Westfall interview.

54. *Vernon*, 7.

55. *Rushville Republican*, 23, 25 July 1970; Al Hodge, interview with Hester Hale, 21 Apr. 1990.

56. *Indianapolis News*, 17 Jan. 1972; *Oldenburg: The Village of Spires* (Indianapolis: Indiana Junior Historical Society, 1970).

57. H. Roll McLaughlin, letter to William T. Alderson, Jr., 31 Jan. 1969, and James C. Massey letter to McLaughin, 21 Jan. 1969, Architectural Survey, 1969–70 file, Indiana Historical Bureau, IJHS Records, Indiana State Archives, Commission on Public Records.

58. *Barns and Other Outbuildings on Indiana Farms* (Indianapolis: Indiana Junior Historical Society, 1975).

59. *Architecture in New Harmony, Indiana, 1814–1969* (New Harmony, Ind.: The Guild, 1969); *19th Century Architecture: Liberty, Indiana* (Liberty, Ind.: Short High School, 1969); *An Architectural and Historical Survey of Switzerland County* (Vevay: Switzerland County Junior Historical Society, 1969); *An Architectural Study and Historic Review of Historic Centerville, Indiana* (Indianapolis: Published for the Chapter by the Indiana Junior Historical Society, 1972); *Architecture along the National Road in Knightstown, Indiana* (Indianapolis: Published for the History Club by the Indiana Junior Historical Society, 1972); *Selected Examples of Nineteenth Century Architecture in Fayette County, Indiana* (Indianapolis: Indiana Junior Historical Society, 1973).

60. *Our River: An Architectural and Historical Journey* (Indianapolis: Indiana Junior Historical Society, 1970), 3.

61. *Louisville Courier-Journal*, 27 June 1969; *Tell City Thursday News*, 26 June 1969.

62. Kathy Cass, notebook of Ohio River cruise, 25 June–2 July 1969, Indiana Historical Bureau, IJHS Records, Indiana State Archives, Commission on Public Records.

63. *History News* 26, no. 8 (Aug. 1971): 168; *Architecture, History, Folklore along the Lincoln Heritage Trail: Springfield, Ky. to Springfield, Ill.* (Indianapolis: Indiana Junior Historical Society, 1970).

64. *An Architectural Journey in Shelbyville and Shelby County: Kentucky, Indiana, and Illinois* (Indianapolis: Indiana Junior Historical Society, 1971), 3.

65. *Selected Examples of Architecture in the Tri-State Area of Indiana, Kentucky, and Illinois* (Indianapolis: Indiana Junior Historical Society, 1972).

66. Robert Montgomery, letter to Charles S. Arthur, 1 Feb. 1964, correspondence file, 1963–64, Indiana Historical Bureau, IJHS Records, Indiana State Archives, Commission on Public Records.

67. *IJHS Newsletter* (16 Nov. 1966).

68. Walter Stephen Pendergast, "An Assessment of the Junior Historian Movement in the United States and Its Implications for Teaching and Learning of State and Local History, 1938–1968" (Ed.D. thesis, Syracuse University, 1974).

69. Lana Ruegamer, *A History of the Indiana Historical Society, 1830–1980* (Indianapolis: Indiana Historical Society, 1980), 281, 283.

70. *Indiana History Bulletin* 53 (Feb. 1976): 19; Marcy Gray, interview with Hester Hale, 11 Apr. 1990.

71. *Vincennes Sun-Commercial,* 10 June 1970.

72. Ibid.

73. *Anderson Daily Bulletin,* 18 Apr. 1970; Gray interview.

74. Indiana Junior Historical Society Alumni Association Constitution, 1969.

75. *Terre Haute Tribune-Star,* 10 Oct. 1971.

76. *Fort Wayne Journal-Gazette,* 13 Feb. 1972.

77. *Terre Haute Tribune-Star,* 10 Oct. 1971.

78. Ibid.; Norm Froderman, letter to Montgomery, 22 Oct. 1971, Wabash & Erie Canal Donations file, Indiana Historical Bureau, IJHS Records, Indiana State Archives, Commission on Public Records; John S. Lynn, letter to Emily Engellund, 1 Mar. 1971, ibid.; John S. Lynn, letter (with $1,000 check enclosed) to Montgomery, 9 Mar. 1971, ibid.; Lilly Endowment, Inc., telephone interview with Hester Hale, 5 Feb. 1990.

79. *Little Hoosier Historian Newsletter* (Mar. 1971).

80. Montgomery, letter to IJHS clubs, 1 Nov. 1971, Indiana Historical Bureau, IJHS Records, Indiana State Archives, Commission on Public Records.

81. Montgomery, letters to Chemical Trust and [Frederick R.] Benson Trust, 3 July 1974, Wabash & Erie Canal file, ibid.

82. Donna Jewel Clark, interview with Hester Hale, 9 Apr. 1990.

83. *Rushville Republican,* 30 Dec. 1977.

84. Claire Carlson, letter to Robert Kirby, 9 May 1974, Indiana Historical Bureau, IJHS Records, Indiana State Archives, Commission on Public Records.

85. Text of award, signed by James Biddle, president of National Trust for Historic Preservation, May 1974, ibid.

Chapter 4

1. *A Handbook for History Club Officers and Sponsors* (Indianapolis, 1966), 13.

2. *IJHS Newsletter* (Sept. 1968).

3. Al Hodge, interview with Hester Hale, 21 Apr. 1990.

4. Robert Montgomery, letter to IJHS officer, 5 July 1967, Special Bulletins file, Indiana Historical Bureau, IJHS Records, Indiana State Archives, Commission on Public Records, Indianapolis; Kevin Stonerock, interview with Hester Hale, 8 Sept. 1989.

5. *History News* 22, no. 5 (May 1967): 112.

6. *A Handbook for History Club Officers and Sponsors,* rev. ed. (Indianapolis: Indiana Junior Historical Society, 1978), 6.

7. Debbie Turpin Fausset, interview with Hester Hale, n.d.

8. *Handbook* (1978), 9, 10; *Handbook* (1966), 9.

9. *IJHS Newsletter* (Dec. 1981).

10. Murray Holliday, introduction to *A View of Ecclesiastical Architecture in Cass County, Indiana* (Indianapolis: Indiana Junior Historical Society, 1972), 3.

11. *IJHS Newsletter* (Sept. 1968).

12. Ibid. (16 Nov. 1966).

13. *Indianapolis Star,* 17 Feb. 1967.

14. *IJHS Newsletter* (16 Nov. 1966).

15. Hodge, interview with Hester Hale, 8 June 1989.

16. Eli Lilly, letter to Mrs. Ruth Lawson, 12 Apr. 1972, Indiana Historical Bureau, IJHS Records, Indiana State Archives, Commission on Public Records.

17. *Muncie Star,* 27 July 1969; Patricia Denker, interview with Hester Hale, 4 Oct. 1989; Dwight Taylor, interviews with Hester Hale, 20 July 1989 and 9 Mar. 1990; enclosure in Robert Kirby letter to Robert H. Everitt (Cornelius O'Brien Fund), 23 May 1977, O'Brien file, Indiana Historical Bureau, IJHS Records, Indiana State Archives, Commission on Public Records.

18. Fausset interview.

19. *Vernon: An Indiana Town, 1968* (Indianapolis: Indiana Junior Historical Society, 1968); *Indiana Countryside, 1968: Walker Township, Rush County* (Indianapolis: Indiana Junior Historical Society, 1968); John N. Hughes, letter to Montgomery, 22 July 1968, Homer Project file, In-

diana Historical Bureau, IJHS Records, Indiana State Archives, Commission on Public Records.

20. Montgomery, letter to William A. Quinn, 10 Oct. 1969, Wabash Project file, Indiana Historical Bureau, IJHS Records, Indiana State Archives, Commission on Public Records.

21. *Nineteenth Century Houses in Wabash, City & County* (Indianapolis: The Society, 1970).

22. Indiana Historical Society, *Annual Report, 1971–1972* (Indianapolis, 1973), 5; Lana Ruegamer, *A History of the Indiana Historical Society, 1830–1980* (Indianapolis: Indiana Historical Society, 1980), 210; *Indiana History Bulletin* 53 (Feb. 1976): 19.

23. *Indiana History Bulletin* 53 (Feb. 1976): 19.

24. *History News* 27, no. 11 (Nov. 1972).

25. Indiana Historical Bureau, personnel records.

26. Thomas Krasean, "A Tribute," *Indiana History Bulletin* 55 (July 1978): 97.

27. Jon Turpin, "A Tribute," ibid., 96.

28. Hubert Hawkins, "Robert Wayne Montgomery, 1907–1978, A Eulogy," ibid., 95.

Chapter 5

1. Kevin Stonerock, interview with Hester Hale, 30 Nov. 1989; Harry Smith, interview with Hester Hale, 7 July 1989; Carl Zenor, interview with Hester Hale, n.d.

2. "House Concurrent Resolution No. 23," first regular session, 99th General Assembly, *Indiana House Journal,* 1975.

3. 1972 Voting Register, IJHS Convention, miscellaneous file, 1970s/1980s, Indiana Historical Bureau, IJHS Records, Indiana State Archives, Commission on Public Records, Indianapolis.

4. "Secretary's Report, Indiana Junior Historical Society, 1986–1987," ibid.

5. Marjorie Snodgrass, telephone interview with Kendal Gladish, 20 Sept. 1996.

6. Candace Taff Carr, interview with Hester Hale, 2 Oct. 1989.

7. Robert Kirby, letter to "Dear Teacher," 14 Apr. 1978.

8. [Robert Kirby] to [teachers' camp staff], 16 Dec. 1981; 18 Mar. 1982, Teachers' Camp file, Indiana Historical Bureau, IJHS Records, Indiana State Archives, Commission on Public Records.

9. *A Handbook for Little Hoosier Historians,* rev. ed. (1986), 12; "Important Information for Little Hoosier Campers," 1974; *Muncie Star,* 24 Oct. 1982; *Little Hoosier Historian Newsletter* (Feb. 1984); Ed and Barbara Johnson, interview with Hester Hale, 25 Feb. 1990.

10. Snodgrass interview.

11. Dwight Taylor, interview with Hester Hale, 19 Mar. 1990.

12. Taylor interview; Jay and Alice Wilson, interview with Hester Hale, 5 Oct. 1989.

13. Evelyn Howell, interview with Hester Hale, 28 Feb. 1990; Taylor interview; Glen Dillman, interview with Hester Hale, 5 May 1990.

14. Marlene Burns, interview with Hester Hale, 21 Mar. 1990.

15. Kathy Koontz, letter to Kirby, 24 Oct. 1978, correspondence file, 1 Aug. 1978–31 July 1979, Indiana Historical Bureau, IJHS Records, Indiana State Archives, Commission on Public Records.

16. Indiana Historical Society, *Annual Report, 1985–1986* (Indianapolis, 1987), 7–8.

17. *Little Hoosier Historian Newsletter,* convention issue [1987].

18. *Revolutionary War Soldiers Buried in Lawrence County, Indiana* (Indianapolis: Published for the Stalker School Little Hoosiers by the Indiana Junior Historical Society, 1978).

19. *History News* 36, no. 11 (Nov. 1981): 27.

20. Harry Smith, interview with Hester Hale, n.d.; *Indianapolis News,* 30 June 1976.

21. Northern Indiana history tour itinerary, 12–17 June 1978.

22. "Secretary's Report, Indiana Junior Historical Society, 1982–1983," Indiana Historical Bureau, IJHS Records, Indiana State Archives, Commission on Public Records.

23. Kevin Stonerock to tour participant, 6 May 1987, Bi-State tour file, ibid.; *Greensburg Daily News,* 10 Aug. 1987.

24. *IJHS Newsletter* (Mar. 1983); *Corydon Democrat,* 22 June 1983.

25. *History News* 35, no. 11 (Nov. 1980): 40.

26. *Indianapolis News,* 3 July 1975, 23 Jan. 1976; "Secretary's Report, Indiana Junior Historical Society, 1975–1976," Indiana Historical Bureau, IJHS Records, Indiana State Archives, Commission on Public Records; *IJHS Newsletter* (Feb. 1979); *Architectural Interpretations as Found in Carroll Counties, Indiana and Kentucky, 1974* (Indianapolis: Indiana Junior Historical Society, 1974); *Along the Highways and Byways of Washington Counties, Kentucky and Indiana* (Indianapolis: Indiana Junior Historical Society, 1975).

27. *Indiana History Bulletin* 56 (Nov. 1979): 160–61; Debbie Turpin Fausset, interview with Hester Hale, n.d.; Stonerock interview.

28. *IJHS Newsletter* (Jan. 1973).

29. *Indiana History Bulletin* 51 (Nov. 1974): 157.

30. Marcy Gray, interview with Hester Hale, n.d.; Donna Jewel Clark, interview with Hester Hale, n.d.

31. "Secretary's Report, 1975–1976"; Gray interview.

32. *IJHS Newsletter* (Nov. 1976).

33. Ibid. (Apr. 1980); Stonerock interview.

34. *IJHS Newsletter* (Apr. 1980); Kampsville Archaeological Field School, 3–9 Aug. 1980, brochure.

35. Stonerock, interview with Hester Hale, 8 Sept. 1989; IJHS Advisory Council Report, 5 Nov. 1977.

36. Debbie Turpin Fausset, letter to Ron Deiss, 22 June 1984, Frankfort Dig file, Indiana Historical Bureau, IJHS Records, Indiana State Archives, Commission on Public Records.

37. Press release, 14 Mar. 1977, Capitol Building Exhibits, 1977 file, Indiana Historical Bureau, IJHS Records, Indiana State Archives, Commission on Public Records; "Secretary's Report, Indiana Junior Historical Society, 1976–1977," ibid.

38. *IJHS Newsletter* (Oct. 1978).

39. Ibid.

40. "George Rogers Clark Symposium, Vincennes University, Vincennes, Indiana, June 19–22, 1979," program, George Rogers Clark Symposium file, Indiana Historical Bureau, IJHS Records, Indiana State Archives, Commission on Public Records; *Indiana History Bulletin* 56 (Aug. 1979): 111.

41. National Endowment for the Humanities Grant Application, 1 June 1978; *IJHS Newsletter* (Apr. 1978); (Feb. 1979).

42. Kirby letter, 17 May 1979, Indiana Historical Bureau, IJHS Records, Indiana State Archives, Commission on Public Records.

43. *Rushville Republican*, 30 Dec. 1977.

44. *Lafayette Journal and Courier*, 28 July 1985; *IJHS Newsletter* (Nov. 1985).

45. *IJHS Newsletter* (Oct. 1967); (Feb. 1978); (Feb. 1980).

46. Ibid. (Sept. 1983).

47. Smith interview; Kirby, letter to [state officers], 5 Oct. 1979, Gettysburg trip, Oct. 25–29, 1979 file, Indiana Historical Bureau, IJHS Records, Indiana State Archives, Commission on Public Records.

48. Jean Gernand, letter to Gayle Thornbrough, 20 Feb. 1979, correspondence file, 1 Aug. 1978–31 July 1979, Indiana Historical Bureau, IJHS Records, Indiana State Archives, Commission on Public Records; *Marion Chronicle-Tribune*, 19 Dec. 1976.

49. *Indiana History Bulletin* 55 (June 1978): 79.

50. *History News* 37, no. 12 (Dec. 1983): 37.

51. *IJHS Newsletter* (Dec. 1978); (Dec. 1979); (Dec. 1980).

52. Ibid. (Nov. 1985); (Sept. 1986); (Sept. 1987); (Sept. 1988).

53. Ron Woodward, interview with Hester Hale, 9 Apr. 1990.

54. Ron Morris, interview with Hester Hale, n.d.; *IJHS Newsletter* (Apr. 1982).

55. Brent Tharp, interview with Hester Hale, 28 Dec. 1989.

56. *Little Hoosier Historian Newsletter* (Nov. 1978).

Chapter 6

1. Lana Ruegamer, *A History of the Indiana Historical Society, 1830–1980* (Indianapolis: Indiana Historical Society, 1980), 302.

2. Ibid., 301.

3. Ibid., 304.

4. *IJHS Newsletter* (Sept. 1981).

5. Ruegamer, *History of the Indiana Historical Society,* 304–11.

6. Thomas Krasean, "Indiana Junior Historical Society, 1989/1990 Survey, Comments/Recommendations—Krasean," p. 1, in Thomas Krasean, memo to Richard Simons and Glen Dillman, 9 Jan. 1990, RG 9, box 14, folder 36, Indiana Historical Society Archives, Indianapolis.

7. Margaret A. Bonney, "Indiana Junior Historical Society Evaluation" (Aug. 1986), 1, folder 39, ibid.

8. Ibid., 10.

9. Ibid., 6–7.

10. Pamela J. Bennett, "Historical Sketch of the Indiana Historical Bureau" (unpublished document, 25 Jan. 1991), Indiana Historical Bureau, IJHS Records, Indiana State Archives, Commission on Public Records, Indianapolis.

11. Bonney, "Indiana Junior Historical Society Evaluation," 15.

12. Ibid., 18.

13. *IJHS Newsletter* (Feb. 1988); (Mar. 1989); Virginia Terpening, interview with Kendal Gladish, 16 May 1996.

14. Krasean, "Indiana Junior Historical Society, 1989/1990 Survey," 1.

15. "Robert W. Kirby, IJHS Director, 1974–1987," *IJHS Newsletter* (Jan. 1988): 1.

16. Kevin Stonerock, interview with Hester Hale, 30 Nov. 1989.

17. Kevin Stonerock, "A Tribute to Mr. Kirby," *IJHS Newsletter* (Jan. 1988): 4.

18. Stonerock interview.

19. IJHS Records; Indiana Historical Society, *Annual Report, 1979–1980* (Indianapolis, 1981); *Annual Report, 1983–1984* (Indianapolis, 1985).

20. *IJHS Newsletter* (Feb. 1986); "Secretary's Report, Indiana Junior Historical Society, 1986–1987," miscellaneous file, Indiana Historical Bureau, IJHS Records, Indiana State Archives, Commission on Public Records.

21. *IJHS Newsletter* (Feb. 1987); "Secretary's Report, 1986–1987"; Stonerock interview.

22. *IJHS Newsletter* (Feb. 1988); (Sept. 1988); Ron Woodward, interview with Hester Hale, n.d.; Stonerock interview.

23. *IJHS Newsletter* (Nov. 1988); Glen Dillman, interview with Hester Hale, n.d.

24. *IJHS Newsletter* (May 1989).

25. Richard Simons, Thomas Krasean, and Glen Dillman, "Indiana Junior Historical Society Survey" (Apr. 1990), and "Report of Ad Hoc Committee on Junior Historical Societies, 18 May 1990," p. 1, RG 9, box 14, folder 35, Indiana Historical Society Archives.

26. "From the Director," and "Thank You Kevin Stonerock . . . and Best of Luck," *The Indiana Junior Historian* (Oct. 1989): 1, 2.

27. Catherine Swanson, "From the Director," ibid. (Nov. 1989): 1.

28. Krasean, "Indiana Junior Historical Society, 1989/1990 Survey," 2.

29. Ibid.

30. Simons, Krasean, and Dillman, "Report of Ad Hoc Committee on Junior Historical Societies," 1.

31. Ibid., 2–3.

32. Indiana Historical Society, "Minutes of the Board of Trustees, Aug. 1990," pp. 3–4, Administration Division, Indiana Historical Society.

33. Ibid.

34. Peter T. Harstad, memo to Pamela J. Bennett, 15 May 1991, Indiana Historical Society Board resolution attachment, Indiana Historical Bureau, IJHS Records, Indiana State Archives, Commission on Public Records.

35. Bennett, memo to Harstad, 22 Apr. 1991, ibid.

36. Simons, Krasean, and Dillman, "Report of Ad Hoc Committee on Junior Historical Societies," 2.

37. "Little Hoosier Summer Camp," *The Indiana Junior Historian* (Mar. 1991): 3.

38. Tony Littell, "To Parents of Little Hoosiers," ibid., 4.

39. Swanson, "From the Director," ibid. (Apr. 1991): 1.

40. Nancy Wolfe, "Dear Junior Historians," *IJHS Newsletter* (Nov. 1991): 1.

Chapter 7

1. "The Soldier's Christmas," *IJHS Newsletter* (Dec. 1991): 1.

2. Nancy Wolfe, interview with Kendal Gladish, 3 Nov. 1997.

3. Nancy Wolfe, written comments on first draft of Chapter 7, 6 Nov. 1997.

4. *IJr.HS Notes* 1, no. 1 (1 Sept. 1992).

5. Wolfe, interviews with Kendal Gladish, 16 May, 20 June 1996, and 3 Nov. 1997.

6. *IJr.HS Notes* 1, no. 3 (1 Nov. 1992): 3.

7. Indiana Junior Historical Society Sponsor Advisory Board, *Exploring the Past through the Eyes of the Future: IJr.HS Handbook for Sponsors* (Indianapolis: Indiana Junior Historical Society, 1993; revised, 1996).

8. Wolfe, written comments.

9. Nancy Wolfe, "Quarterly Report, Indiana Junior Historical Society," August 1993, Administration Division, Indiana Historical Society.

10. *IJr.HS Notes* 2, no. 1 (1 Sept. 1993): 6.

11. Wolfe, written comments.

12. Nancy Wolfe, "IJr.HS Honors Youths and Sponsors at State Convention," *The Bridge* 2, no. 5 (Sept.–Oct. 1996): 10; Wolfe interview, 3 Nov. 1997.

13. Wolfe, written comments.

14. Wolfe, "Quarterly Report, Indiana Junior Historical Society," July 1997.

15. Wolfe, written comments.

16. *IJr.HS Notes* 2, no. 1 (1 Sept. 1993): 5; Wolfe, "Quarterly Report, Indiana Junior Historical Society," 13 Oct. 1993; July 1997.

17. Wolfe, written comments.

18. Ibid.

19. *IJr.HS Notes* 1, no. 4 (1 Dec. 1992): 6.

20. Wolfe, written comments.

21. Grant F. Goshorn, "What a Quarter Can Buy," *The Bridge* 3, no. 6 (Nov.–Dec. 1997): 5.

22. Wolfe, "Quarterly Report, Indiana Junior Historical Society," Oct. 1996.

23. Ibid., 11 Oct. 1994.

24. Ibid., Oct. 1996.

25. Ibid., July 1997.

26. Ibid., July 1996.

27. Wolfe, written comments.

28. Wolfe, "Quarterly Report, Indiana Junior Historical Society," 4 Apr. 1997.

29. Wolfe interview, 3 Nov. 1997; ibid., written comments.

30. Paula Beeson, interview with Kendal Gladish, 11 May 1996.

31. Wolfe, written comments.

Appendix

State Presidents of the Indiana Junior
Historical Society

1938–39   (acting) Fred I. Jones, Shortridge High School
1939–40   John D. Williams, Arsenal Technical High School
1940–41   Henrietta Parrish, Bloomington High School
1941–42   Edward C. McKinney, Arsenal Technical High School
1942–43   James Keenan, Washington High School
1943–44   Gwendolyn Jackson, Warren Central High School
1944–45   Norman Nelson, Warren Central High School
1945–50   no state officers
1950–51   Cortes Perry, Columbus High School
1951–52   Jerry McAvoy, Tipton High School
1952–53   Sue Jay, Decatur Central High School
1953–54   Jon Myers, Lebanon High School
1954–55   David Adams
1955–56   Dick Harden, Fortville High School
1956–57   Russel Duvall, Decatur Central High School
1957–58   Charles Stalcup, Broad Ripple High School
1958–59   Martha Fulford, Martinsville High School
1959–60   Webster Wright, Broad Ripple High School
1960–61   Joyce Allen, Sandcreek High School
1961–62   Information not available

1962–63   Dee Ann Holloway, Washington High School
1963–64   Roger Chaffin, Broad Ripple High School
1964–65   Mary Jane Hollcraft, Marion High School
1965–66   John Walling, Mount Vernon High School
1966–67   Anna Jane Miller, Wes-Del High School
1967–68   Judy Lewis, Manual High School
1968–69   Dyan Bricker, Oak Hill High School
1969–70   John Wyatt, Elmhurst High School
1970–71   Keith Shallenberger, Haworth High School
1971–72   Janet Wolfgang, Pennville High School
1972–73   Gene Hinshaw, Morristown High School
1973–74   Michael Lynch, Brownsburg High School
1974–75   Jon Turpin, Knightstown High School
1975–76   Hal E. Page, Howe High School
1976–77   Sam Swearingen, Whitewater Valley High School
1977–78   Debbie Campbell, Connersville High School
1978–79   Doug Jewel, DeKalb County Junior High School
1979–80   Brian Crume, Carroll High School
1980–81   Bill Maxam, South Vigo High School
1981–82   Brent Tharp, Mary Bryan Pioneers
1982–83   Cindy Souder, Rushville High School
1983–84   Steve Turpin, Knightstown High School
1984–85   Lisa Ulrich, Whitewater Valley High School
1985–86   Mike Mohr, Rushville High School

1986–87	Leah Flora, Carroll High School, and Melanie Stone, Hauser High School	1992–93	David Roberts, North Central High School
1987–88	Bobby Waddle, Hauser High School	1993–94	Jonathan Sager, Carroll Junior-Senior High School
1988–89	Bill Johnson, Hauser High School	1994–95	Todd Froedge, Hauser High School
1989–90	Amy Moore, Hauser High School	1995–96	Todd Froedge, Hauser High School
1990–91	Amy Carr, Columbus North High School	1996–97	Claire Carr, Cardinal Ritter High School
1991–92	Laura Lewis, Columbus East High School	1997–98	Grant Goshorn, Columbus East High School
		1998–99	Erin Moore, Danville High School

Index

Ad Hoc Committee on Junior Historical Societies, 88, 91, 92
Adams, John, 74
Adams Mill, 5, 74, 77
Allen County–Fort Wayne Historical Society, 36, 57
Allen County Historical Museum, 38
Allen County Junior Historical Society, 6, 36
American Association for State and Local History (AASLH), 60, 68, 69, 77
American Camping Association (ACA), 98
American Girl (magazine), 47
American Institute of Architects, 42
Ammonett, Andrew, 85
Angel Mounds, 64
Angel Site: An Archaeological, Historical, and Ethnological Site, 44
Anthony Wayne Club (Fort Wayne), 20, 25
Arbuckle, Kathryn, 25
The Archaeological Investigations of Fort Knox II, 44
Archer, Mrs. Guy, 46
Arlington High School (Indianapolis), 35, 38
Arsenal Technical High School (Indianapolis), 16, 17, 19, 20, 25; illus., 15

Artis, Tammy, 6; illus., 11
Aurora, 19

Bailey, J. J., 33
Bardstown (Ky.), 68
Barns and Other Outbuildings on Indiana Farms, 42
Batesville, 68
Battle Ground, 69
Beech Grove High School, 20
Beeson, Jessica, 105, 107; illus., 103
Beeson, Paula, 105
Belle of Louisville, 100
Ben Davis High School (Indianapolis), 36
Bennett, Pamela J., 81, 84, 85, 88, 91; illus., 83
Benton County, 42
Bertels, Glenn: illus., 37
Bessie Keeran Roberts Award, 57
Beverly Shores, 102
Biddle, James: illus., 76
Billie Creek Village, 100
Black, Glenn A., 44, 46
Bob Montgomery Memorial Award, 80
Bonney, Margaret A., 82, 84

Brademas, John, 77
Brady, Mathew, 5
Branigin, Roger D., 36
Bray, William, 47; illus., 45
Bricker, Dyan, 39; illus., 37
A Brief Guide Book for an Architectural Survey of Indiana, 39
Briggs, Herbert, 13
Broad Ripple High School (Indianapolis), 17
Broadhurst, Jim, 74
BROADSIDES, 82
Brown, Foster, 102
Brown, Rosalie, 2
Brush Creek Elementary School, 6
Bulletin: Indiana Junior Historical Society, 18
Bultman, Russ, 38
Burkesville (Ky.), 68
Burns, Marlene, 67; illus., 71

Calumet Region, 102
Cambridge City, 70, 73, 77
Cammeck's Mill, 73
Canada, 100
Carl J. Polk Little Hoosiers Club, 5, 97

Carnighan, Mike, 38

Carr, Candy Taff, 97; illus., 66, 95

Carroll, Horace Bailey, 16

Carroll County, 69, 74

Carroll County Junior-Senior Historians: and log cabin restoration, 1; illus., 3

Carroll County log cabin, 87; illus., 90

Carroll County Museum, 5

Carroll Historians, 74, 87

Cass County, 42, 60

Cassidy, Joanna: illus., 83

Catron, George B., 2

Catron, Steve, 1; illus., 8

Centerville, 43

A Century of Development: Grant County, Indiana, 14

Challenger Learning Center (Brownsburg), 100

Chambers, Joyce, 88

Charleston (Ill.), 43

Chief Richardville Home, 77

"The Civil War in Song" (program), 80

Clark, Charles: illus., 76

Clark, George Rogers, 74

Clarke, Benny, 36

Cliocrat Club (University High School, Bloomington), 17

Coleman, Christopher B., 14, 17, 19, 20, 23; illus., 15

Columbus, 92

Columbus East High School, 100

Columbus High School, 25

Columbus Northside Junior High School, 36, 38

Columbus Youth Camp, 92, 98

Commission for the Reorganization of School Corporations, 30

Commission of General Education, 32

Committee on Junior Historical Organizations, 17, 22

Conklin House (Cambridge City), 41

Conner Prairie Junior Historical Society, 97

Conner Prairie Pioneer Settlement, 78

Connersville, 43, 77

Corydon, 68

Cramer, Debbie, 33

Crawford County, 69

Crawfordsville, 69

"Curing Meat in the Home" (program), 80

Current Cemetery: cleanup, 1; illus., 7

Cutler, 5, 74

Daleville, 87

Dau, William, 17

Decatur Central History Club, 25

Deiss, Ron, 73

De Kalb County, 42

Dell, Homer, 41

Denker, Patricia, 59

Department of Public Instruction, 13, 20; and social studies curriculum, 30

Dillman, Glen, 2, 5, 67, 68, 74, 87, 88, 97; illus., 8, 79, 89

Director's Trophy, 54, 59, 80

Directory of Historical Markers, 1, 36

Doan, Deborah, 38

Doup, Carol Lynn, 38

Driscoll, Jearl, 93

Dunn, Walter, 17

Dye, Charity, 10; illus., 12

Edison Historians, 97

Edison Junior-Senior High School (Lake Station), 97

Edson, Margo, 36, 38

Emison, Thomas S., 32

English, William H., 9

Ernie Pyle State Historic Site, 100

"Events in the Lives of Common Folk" (program), 80

"Exploring and Teaching . . . Indiana's Ohio River Valley," 102

Falls of the Ohio State Park, 100

Farnham Scholarship, 54

Fausset, Debbie Turpin, 62, 77, 80, 85, 107; illus., 58, 79

Fentress, William (Billy Yank), 85

Ferdinand, 59

Festival of the Arts (Homer), 41

Fish, Bill, 36

Flora, 1

Flora History Club: illus., 34

Flora Park, 87

Ford Meter Box Company, 60

Fort Knox II, 1; archaeology dig, 46, 60; illus., 4

Fort Ouiatenon: archaeology dig, 44; illus., 40

Fort Wayne, 68, 77

Fort Wayne Central High School, 16, 25

Fortney, Mary, 9

Fountain Central High School, 36, 38

Frankfort (Ky.), 73

Franklin County Traveling Trophy, 54

Frederick R. Benson Trust, 47

French House (Vincennes): archaeology dig, 73; illus., 72

Funk, Arville: illus., 31

Garmon, Harry O., 17

Gen. Lew Wallace Study, 69

Geography Educators Network of Indiana (GENI), 102

George Rogers Clark Symposium, 74; participants illus., 76

George Washington High School (Indianapolis), 16, 17, 19, 20, 25

Gernand, Jean: illus., 76

Gillogly, Patricia, 94, 100, 102, 105; illus., 95, 103

Goddard School: restoration, 1, 45, 47, 48, 63, 74; illus., 3, 45

"The Goddard School Restoration," 80

Goldstein, Alan: illus., 101

Gordon, Robert W., 32, 33

Goshorn, Grant, 100, 107; illus., 99

Governor's Cup, 54

Grant County Junior Historical Society, 14, 16

Gray, Marlesa (Marcy), 44, 70, 73; illus., 72

Gray, Vicki, 36

Greene, Jim, 38

Griest, Alva C., 93

Harrel, Mrs. Samuel: illus., 53

Harrison, William Henry, 19, 38, 78

Harrison Township High School (Delaware County), 29, 36

Harstad, Peter T., 82, 91; illus., 86

Haupt, Richard, 24, 25

Hauser Junior-Senior High Historians, 6

Hawkins, Hubert H., 25, 27, 29, 32, 33, 35, 59, 60, 62, 81; illus., 21, 26

Hayden Historical Museum, 1

Hayden Little Hoosiers: and restoration work, 1; illus., 4

Head, Molly, 38

Heller, Herbert, 25

Hendricks, Polly, 41

Henry County, 42, 69

Historical Markers and Public Memorials in Indiana (1929), 36

History Cruiser II, 100

"History for Young People: Organizing a Junior Society," 60

History News, 60

"History on Wheels," 59; illus., 55

Hobart Historians, 97

Hodge, Al, 41, 57; illus., 53

Holmes, John, 38

"At Home in Indiana" (TV program), 74

"Home Remedies" (program), 80

Homer, 1, 41, 47, 60

Honeywell Foundation, 60

Hook, William H., 100

Hoosier Historian, 22, 23, 24, 49, 50, 57

Hoosier State Bank (Hammond), 46

Hope, 6

Houchins, Brenda, 85

House Bill 1094 (1967), 32

House Concurrent Resolution No. 23, p. 63

Howe High School (Indianapolis), 17

Howell, Evelyn, 67; illus., 66

Hubbard, Jon, 41

Hudnut, William H., III, 47; illus., 45

"Hunting Hoosier History," 36

Huntington North Junior Historical Society: wins national award, 77

Indiana Arts Commission, 102

Indiana Chemical Trust, 47

Indiana Council for Social Studies, 102

Indiana Department of Conservation, 24

Indiana Department of Education, 9

Indiana Department of Public Instruction, 10

Indiana Dunes National Lakeshore, 102

Indiana Dunes State Park, 98, 100

Indiana General Assembly, 9, 27; and reorganization of school districts, 27, 30; and mandatory Indiana history course, 32; creates Sesquicentennial Commission, 35; and funding for Indiana Junior Historical Society, 35, 84; congratulates Indiana Junior Historical Society for services and achievements, 63

Indiana Has Almost Everything (film), 22

Indiana Historical Bureau, 9, 10, 17, 42, 44, 49, 60; finances Indiana Junior Historical Society newsletter, 23; Indiana Junior Historical Society field agent put on payroll of, 24; appeals to General Assembly for funds for Indiana Junior Historical Society, 27; employs full-time director for Indiana Junior Historical Society, 29; enlists Indiana Junior Historical Society's aid in historical marker program, 36; changes in and effect of on Indiana Junior Historical Society, 81, 82; and funding and administration of Indiana Junior Historical Society, 82, 84, 91, 92; drops session of Indiana Junior Historical Society camp, 87

Indiana Historical Commission, 9, 10, 13, 81; illus., 12

Indiana Historical Society, 9, 13, 17, 20, 35, 38, 43, 44, 46, 57, 60; and establishment of Indiana Junior Historical Society, 14, 16; conferences, 16, 17, 20, 77; and funding of Indiana Junior Historical Society, 27, 82; contributes to salary of Indiana Junior Historical Society director, 29; awards scholarship, 54; changes in and effect of on Indiana Junior Historical Society, 81, 82; expansion of programs, 82; and financial and administrative support of Indiana Junior Historical Society, 82, 84, 91, 92; forms ad hoc committee on junior historical societies, 88; reorganization of, 94; new headquarters, 105; illus., 104

Indiana Historical Society School Committee, 25

Indiana history: teaching of in schools, 9, 10, 13, 30, 32, 33, 35, 63

Indiana History Bulletin, 16, 18, 20, 33, 36

Indiana History Conference, 13, 16, 17, 23

Indiana History Workshop, 24

Indiana Humanities Council, 102

Indiana Junior Historical Society: cemetery cleanup, 1–2; and restorations, 1, 5, 47, 74, 77, 87; publications, 1, 14, 18, 22, 23, 36, 39, 41, 42, 43, 44, 49, 69, 88, 102; architectural surveys, 1, 39, 41, 42, 43, 44, 60, 69, 70, 98; archaeology digs, 1, 70, 73, 87–88; illus., 4, 10, 44, 46; conventions, 2, 14, 15, 16, 17, 19, 20, 24, 25, 50, 54, 78, 97, 98, 102, 105; illus., 51–53, 96; importance of sponsors, 5, 9, 27, 57, 64; camp, 5, 59, 64, 67, 70, 87; and curriculum development and revisions, 9, 10, 27, 30, 32, 33; establishment of, 13, 14; elections, 16, 17, 19, 39, 54, 80; and constitutions, 16, 17, 29, 50, 94; Indiana Historical Society and Indiana Historical Bureau expectations of, 17; World War II affects, 19; postwar revival and reorganization, 20, 22, 23; and awards and contests, 20, 22, 25, 54, 57, 80, 94, 97, 98; pin, 23; illus., 26; field representative,
24, 25, 102; gets full-time, state-funded director, 29; and creation of junior high clubs, 29–30; and effects of school redistricting and consolidation on, 30; establishes Little Hoosier chapters, 33; first Little Hoosier chapter chartered, 33; and Indiana Sesquicentennial, 35, 36, 38; and teacher workshops, 35, 57, 64, 102; and funding of, 35, 60, 82, 84; and fund-raising activities, 35–36, 46, 47, 98; aids Indiana Historical Bureau's historical marker program, 36; pilgrimages/tours, 38, 42, 59, 64, 68, 69, 77, 87, 88, 100; interstate activities, 44, 50, 69–70, 73, 74, 77; handbook, 49, 94, 97; cemetery records searched, 50, 69; workshops, 50, 70, 77, 78, 88, 100, 105; political activism, 63; and high school membership, 63; recruitment of clubs, 64; growth of, 68; and AASLH awards, 68, 69, 77; oral history projects, 69; participation in centennial of General Assembly, 74; exhibitions, 74, 97; shared club activities, 77; club wins national award, 77; awards to clubs, 78, 80; programs for clubs, 80; evaluation of, 84; camp session cut, 87; and financial and administrative support from Indiana Historical Society and Indiana Historical Bureau, 91, 92; moves camp site, 92, 98; combines conventions of Little Hoosier and junior-senior divisions, 97; camp attendance, 98; video journal, 100; research and essay project, 98, 100; outreach efforts, 102; number of chapters, 102, 105. *See also* Little Hoosier Historians

Indiana Junior Historical Society Advisory Board, 30, 94, 102

Indiana Junior Historical Society Alumni Association, 39, 46, 47, 78, 80, 88, 107

Indiana Junior Historical Society Christmas Gathering, 87

IJHS Newsletter, 36, 38, 49, 74

IJr.HS Notes, 102

Indiana Junior Historical Society Pioneer Festival, 78

Indiana Junior Historical Society Sesquicentennial Committee, 35, 36, 38

"The IJHS—What Is It?" (program), 80

Indiana Library and Historical Board, 25, 29, 32

Indiana Medical History Museum, 102

Indiana Sesquicentennial Commission, 29, 36

Indiana State Library, 9, 24, 36, 50, 78, 102

Indiana State Library and Historical Building, 82

Indiana State Museum, 57, 93

Indiana State Teachers Association (ISTA), 10

Indiana Teacher-Student History Convention, 14, 15

Indiana University Foundation, 22, 25

Indianapolis, 68

Indianapolis Public School 82, p. 62

Indianapolis Public School 110, pp. 5, 64

Indianapolis Star, 10

Indianapolis Star Magazine, 23

James Associates, 47

Jarvis, Martha, 38

Jasper, 59

Jay County, 42, 70

Jefferson County, 42

Jefferson Proving Grounds, 69

Jeffersonville, 69

Jewel, Donna, 62

John Conner Junior Historical Society, 69
John H. Holliday Award, 57
John Strange Elementary School (Indianapolis), 6, 97
John Strange School History Club, 20
Johnson, Julie, 41
Jones, Fred, 16
Jones, James R., III, 73
The Junior Historian, 18
Junior historical movement, 16, 60
Junior History Bulletin, 18
"A Junior Sampler" (exhibition), 97

Kampsville (Ill.), 73, 88
Kampsville One-Week Archaeological Workshop, 73
Kekionga, 77
Kellar, James H., 44
Kelsay, Mary: illus., 76
Kentuckiana, 50, 77
Kentucky Junior Historical Society, 69, 73, 77
Kentucky Young Historians, 43, 44, 50
Kirby, Robert, 47, 62, 63, 64, 68, 69, 70, 74, 77, 78, 80, 81, 82, 84, 85, 94; illus., 45, 58, 79
Knights of History (Arlington High School), 38
Knightstown, 43
Knightstown High School History Club, 2
Kokomo High School, 36
Koontz, Kathy, 67
Krasean, Thomas K., 36, 38, 42, 62, 82, 85, 88, 91, 94; illus., 86
Kuykendall, Ronald L., 25

Ladd, Roy, 74; illus., 76

Lafayette, 44
Lafayette Jefferson High School, 16
Lake Station, 5, 97
Lanier Mansion (Madison), 1
Larimore, Deb, 102
Laurel, 77
Laurel, A Hoosier Community, 69
Lawrence County, 69
Lawson, Earl: illus., 37
Lawson, Ruth, 57
Leavenworth, 69
Lebanon High School, 25
Leiters Ford, 87
Lennox, Nancy: illus., 55
Liberty, 43
Lilly, Eli, 9, 44, 57, 59, 81; bequest to Indiana Historical Society, 81, 82; company, 81; illus., 55
Lilly Endowment, 47, 60, 80
Lincoln, Abraham, 43
Lincoln, Thomas, 43
Lincoln Boyhood National Memorial, 64
Lincoln Heritage Trail, 43
Lincoln State Park, 59
Lindley, Harlow, 10
Lions Club (Riley): aids Indiana Junior Historical Society project, 46
Lisbon (Ohio), 68
Littell, Tony, 92
Little Hoosier Camp, 59, 70, 88, 98, 92; illus., 56
Little Hoosier Historians, 32, 33, 35, 57, 59, 88; publish student writings, 50; workshop, 54; organization of, 59; tours, 59; chapters increase, 63, 68
Little Hoosier Leadership Award, 57
Little Hoosier Pioneer Arts and Crafts camp,

59, 64
Lockport: archaeology dig, 47, 63; illus., 40
Lockridge, Ross Franklin, 16, 22
Loomis, Marilyn, 23, 25
LTV Steel, 98, 100
Lynn, 97, 105

McConnell, Abby, 2; illus., 8
McDowell, Marcy, 47, 107; illus., 45
McKinney, Edward, Jr., 18, 19
McLaughlin, H. Roll, 43
Madame C. J. Walker Theatre, 102
Madison, 39, 43
Madison County, 69
"Making a Slide Program or Filmstrip of Your Community's History," 97
"Making Rawhide and a Dugout Canoe" (program), 80
Marcellino, Dana, 2; illus., 8
Marion High School, 14, 16, 17
Martin, Joseph, 25
Mary Bryan Pioneers (Southport), 78
Meeker, Mary Jane, 102
Meredith, Solomon, 70
Meritorious Service Award, 57
Metamora, 77
Michigan City, 100
Michigan City Public Library, 102
Midwest Conference of Junior Historians, 44
Miller, Anna Jane, 36; illus., 37
Miller, Gene, 47
Miller, Lotus, 47
Miller, Rue, 47
Milton, 73
Mississinewa Battleground, 16
Modoc, 1

Montgomery, Pauline, 62, 73, 77; illus., 72
Montgomery, Robert J., 29, 35, 36, 39, 41, 42, 43, 44, 47, 49, 50, 57, 59, 60, 62, 64, 69, 73, 77, 80, 81, 82, 98, 107; eulogies, 62; illus., 31, 37, 52, 55, 61
Moore, Allison, 107
Moore, Christopher, 2; illus., 8
Moore, Mary Elizabeth, 20
Morgan, John Hunt, 68
"Morgan's Raid of 1863," p. 80
Morocco High School, 25
Morris, Ron, 88; illus., 90
Morris-Butler House (Indianapolis), 102
Mounds State Park, 87
Mt. Healthy Elementary School (Columbus), 92
Mount Vernon, 43
Mount Vernon High School, 42
Muncie, 87
Muncie Central High School, 38
Muscatatuck Park (Jennings County), 5, 59, 64, 70, 87, 88, 92
Muscatatuck Summer History Workshop, 70
Muscatatuck Work Camp, 70

Nasser, Beverly: illus., 31
National History Day, 82
National Junior Historian Newsletter, 39, 44, 49, 50
National Park Service, 42
National Society of Colonial Dames, Indiana chapter, 9, 50, 54, 57
National Trust for Historic Preservation, 47, 77
Neeley, Kenneth, 36, 38
Neeves, Glenn: illus., 31
New Albany, 69, 100

New Albany Junior Historical Society and Nature Study Club, 14
New Harmony, 43, 64
New Harmony Guild of Guides, 36, 42
"Nineteenth Century Architecture" (program), 80
Noblesville, 78
Noblesville Junior High School, 38
Noggle, Anne, 2
Norman, Marjorie, 17
North Central High School (Indianapolis), 97
North Manchester, 69
North Posey High School, 42
Notes on Indiana, 50

Oakland Farm: archaeological dig, 70; illus., 72
O'Bannon, Robert, 29; illus., 31
Old Jail Museum (Crawfordsville), 69
Oldenburg, 41
Oldenburg: The Village of Spires, 41
Oliver, John W., 13
One Hundred Years of Lawrence County, Indiana, Architecture, 69
Orrahood, Susie, 44
Outstanding Club Trophy, 59

Parke County, 100
Parrish, Henrietta, 17
Patton, Mary Alice, 25
Paxson, Fred, 70
Paxson farm, 70, 73
Peat, Wilbur D., 39
Peckham, Howard H., 20, 23, 24, 25; illus., 21
Pennville, 70

Perkinsville, 87
Peru High School, 36
Petersburg, 59
Pierian Club (Columbus), 25
Pinhook Bog, 102
Pitts, Larry, 102
Pomeroy (Ohio), 68
Posey County, 42
Puccini, Libero, 2

Ramsey, Mrs. ____: illus., 37
Randolph County Junior-Senior High School (Lynn), 2, 105
Randolph Southern Junior-Senior High School (Lynn), 97
REACH (program), 82
Reeder, Jane, 25
Remy, William H., 18
Reorganization Act (schools), 30
Richardville, Jean Baptiste, 77
Riley, 46
Riley, James Whitcomb, 38
Roberts, Bessie Keeran, 57
Roberts, David, 6, 107; illus., 11, 86
Rochester, 87
Rockport, 59
Ross, Louise, 19
Rossville Junior High School, 38
Rough River (Ky.), 50
Ruddick, Rodger: illus., 4
Rush County, 41, 60
Rush County Historical Society, 60
Rushville High School, 41, 48, 77
Rushville Junior High School, 38

Sandcreek High School (Decatur County), 26
Savage, Stephen, 24
School District Reorganization Act (1959), 27
Scott County, 42
Seehausen, Paul, 20, 22
Sell, William, 14
Sesquicentennial Commission, 35
Shelby, Isaac, 43
Shelby County (Ill.), 43
Shelby County (Ind.), 43
Shelby County (Ky.), 43
Shelbyville (Ill.), 43
Shelbyville (Ind.), 43
Shelbyville (Ky.), 43
Shiloh National Military Park, 100
Shiloh project, 98, 100; illus., 99
Shortridge High School (Indianapolis), 14, 16, 17, 20
Shortridge High School History Club, 20
Simons, Richard S., 14, 16, 17, 20, 22, 23, 24, 88, 107; wins AASLH award, 60; illus., 15
Slocum, Frances, 16
Smith, Edgar B., 32
Smith, Harry, 68, 77
Smith, Judy, 6; illus., 11
Snodgrass, Marjorie, 5, 64
Social Science Club of Arsenal Technical High School (Indianapolis), 20
Social Studies Club of Arsenal Technical High School (Indianapolis), 17
Society of Indiana Pioneers, 9, 42, 57, 60; contributes to salary of Indiana Junior Historical Society director, 29
Southeastern Indiana Water Crossing Survey, 60
Spencer, 69
Sponsor Advisory Board, 91

Spring Mill, 69
"Spring Mill State Park," 80
Stalker Little Hoosiers (Bedford), 68
Stallings, Prudence, 36
State Board of Education, 10, 13, 32
State Social Studies Curriculum Revision Committee, 32
State Superintendent of Public Instruction, 13
Statehouse Exhibit, 74; illus., 75
Stephenson, D. C., 18
Stonerock, Kevin, 2, 80, 82, 85, 87, 88, 94, 102, 107; illus., 7, 65, 89
Stonycreek Farm, 78
Swanson, Catherine, 88, 92, 93; illus., 90
Sycamore Club (Carroll County), 2, 97

Taylor, Dwight, 67; illus., 55, 66, 86
Taylor, Robert M., Jr., 94; illus., 95
Teachers' Tour of Southwestern Indiana, 64
Terpening, Virginia, 85, 92; illus., 86
Texas: organization of junior historical society in, 16
Thom, Abby, 107
Thornbrough, Gayle, 22, 24, 81, 82; illus., 21, 83
Tipton History Hunters, 100
Tolley, Sharon, 38
Trevlac, 98
Turkey Run State Park, 100
Turner, Ann: illus., 37
Turpin, Debbie. See Fausset, Debbie Turpin
Turpin, Joe, 74
Turpin, Jon, 62, 107; illus., 3

Underground Railroad, 100

Union Elementary School, 1
Union Little Hoosiers: and restoration of log house, 1; illus., 4
United States Air Force Museum (Dayton, Ohio), 100
University High School (Bloomington), 16, 17

Van Buren, Martin, 78
Vanderburgh County, 44
Vanderstel, Sheryl, 84
Vernon, 60
Vernon Junior Historical Society, 41
Versailles, 69
Versailles, A Small Indiana Town, 1818–1976, p. 69
Vevay, 43
A View of Ecclesiastical Architecture of Cass County, 42
Vigo County, 46
Vincennes, 38, 43, 44, 46, 59, 64, 68, 74

W. D. Little Hoosiers (Columbus), 97
Wabash, 60
Wabash and Erie Canal, 46
Wabash County, 60
Wabash County Historical Society, 60
Wabash Junior High. See Wabash Middle School
Wabash Middle School, 6, 77
Wabash Middle School History Club, 68
Wabash Plain Dealer, 60
Walker Township School District No. One, 47
Walnut Hills Retreat (Brown County), 98
"The War Is Over" (program), 2
Warren Central High School (Indianapolis), 17, 19, 20

Warren Central History Club, 20
Warsaw Community School Corporation, 5
Warsaw High School, 20
Washburn, Virginia, 16
Washington County, 69
Wayne County, 73
Weaver, Susie, 62
Weisner, Joann, 105
Wells, Herman B, 17
Westfall, Mike, 6, 36, 38, 39, 107; illus., 11, 53
Westwood School (Batesville): first chartered
    Little Hoosier chapter, 33
Whitcomb, Edgar, 1

Whitewater Canal, 73, 77
Whitewater Valley club, 62
Whitewater Valley Junior Historical Society, 77
Wiley High School (Terre Haute), 46
Williams, Fred, 5, 98; illus., 8
Williams, John D., 17
Williams, Oscar H., 13, 14
Williamson, Johnie, 38
Wilson, Alice: illus., 90
Wilson, Jay, 62, 67, 68, 87; illus., 61, 89
Wilson, William E., 30, 32, 38
Winger, Otho, 19
Wolfe, Nancy, 5, 92, 93, 94, 97, 98, 100, 102,

105; illus., 8, 95
Woodward, Ron, 5, 10, 68; illus., 11
WOWO (radio), 36, 38
Wren, Christopher, 42
WTTV, 74

Young, Wilbur, 23, 24
Young Audiences of Indiana, 102

Zenor, Carl, 25, 29, 35, 77

DATE DUE

NOV 0 1 '99			

DEMCO 38-297